HAPPY BIRTHDAY C

HAVE A GREAT DAY, AN

MANY BLESSINGS AS STARS IN THE SKY

ENJOY THIS BOOK WITH THE FREEDOM
OF A EAGLES WINGS

KEITH xxx .

THE SHAMAN'S
GARDEN
MEMORIES STOLEN
FROM THE DEAD STARS

School of Life Press

꧁ꦽꦽꦽꦽꦽꦽꦽꦽꦽꦽꦽꦽꦽꦽꦽꦽꦽꦽ꧂

THE SHAMAN'S GARDEN
MEMORIES STOLEN
FROM THE DEAD STARS

A BRANCH OF TOLTEC SHAMANISM

IZCOATL PAPLOTZIN
(AGUSTÍN)

WITH FOREWORD BY VÍCTOR SÁNCHEZ
TRANSLATION BY JOANNA CROWSON

꧁ꦽꦽꦽꦽꦽꦽꦽꦽꦽꦽꦽꦽꦽꦽꦽꦽꦽꦽ꧂

The Shaman's Garden
 Memories Stolen from the Dead Stars
A Branch of Toltec Shamanism

A book from School of Life Press

Publishing History
First published in Spain by mtm editores 2002, reprinted 2003
This edition translated by Joanna Crowson and published in Britain by
School of Life Press, 2004

© Itzcoatl Papalotzin, 2004

Cover design by Jesús de Mula G. de R.
Interior design by Jesús de Mula G. de R.
Typeset by Graphicsol, Conil, Cádiz, Spain
Printed and bound in Spain by Graphicsol
ISBN 84-609-1035-0

For information contact:
School of Life Press,
C/Lanería 1,
11150 Vejer de la Frontera,
Cádiz, Spain
Tel/Fax +34 956 447637
www.school-of-life.net
mail@school-of-life.net

*"The light years that exist between Andromeda and ourselves
is a myth that people believe in, because
Andromeda is in us and we are in her."*

David Cooper

*"And what would you do... if God spoke directly to your face
and said, 'I command that you be happy in the world,
as long as you live.' What would you do then?"*

Richard Bach

CONTENTS

ACKNOWLEDGEMENTS

To those who taught me to think for myself and not to believe every-thing the world says: to Jaime, my brother, to Mariví, my energetic mother, to Víctor Sánchez, to Carlos Aranda Castaneda.

To those who cared for me when I was a human pup.

To those who make up my biological family: my mother, Jaime, Pablo, Ivonne, Sandra, Eli, my cousin Ivan and my aunt Deya, and also to my energetic family who are more than I can count.

To those who helped me buy the Casita, clean it and make it into what it is: Camen Yoldi, Petra Schutler and Matías, Clara de la Gandara, Iris Martínez Paz Pocahonta, Inma, Ramón Herrero, Sor Vito, and to all those who were in the house that first summer.

To her, who I only see in my dreams.

To Montse Canellas, for giving me the pleasure of appearing in my life.

To my organizers and friends, Verena González, Adela Escudero, Ulla, Karola Beltram, Angi, Tina, Ju; to Manolo Pablo, Luis 'Manolito' Ibarra, Noemi and Birdi, Dagmar, Renata Sprenz and Regine Probst.

To Jaume Codina, for being an exceptional guardian angel.

To Lucy Santoro, my beloved wife, who has taught me what recti-tude is, for opening the doorway in my soul to purity and fulfilment as a man.

To Esperanza Yoldi, for her unconditional support and her example to others.

To Joanna Crowson, who enlarges the world with her strength and spirituality.

To Paco Zarate, Danna Rebasa and José María.

To Pamela Ann Fields (Tania), for that wonderful time we lived together.

To my apprentices in Andalusia, especially Christopher Davidson (also known as Christopher Robinson), Merry and Daisy, Jesús de Mula and Paquy Cano, Jorge and Manuelita, and to my great friend Luis 'Toc Toc' Puerta, Chari and Minerva.

To my English-speaking pupils, especially Francesca Vandelli, Esther, Sophia, Ken and Hilda, for appearing in my life and inspiring me to produce this English version.

To me for being who I want to be and for having kept myself alive.

FOREWORD BY VÍCTOR SÁNCHEZ

I have known Edgar (or Agustín as he is known in Europe) for almost 30 years. We shared our path of growth when we were just boys with fantastic dreams in our heads and a disposition for adventure and daring in our hearts.

While very young we founded 'The Other Sorcery' and its later manifestation, 'The Art of Living Purposefully'. In this organisation we offered activities and gave workshops in which the joy we found in nature blended with our love for indigenous knowledge and our passion for human development.

Whilst I liked magic but was passionate about research, Edgar liked research but was passionate about magic. From 1983 to 1993, within the dream called The Art of Living Purposefully, we walked the path together, exploring, learning, teaching and enjoying ourselves in river, jungle, forest, desert, sea and mountain. Together we led many people on this new path towards personal and spiritual growth. Then we separated. We each had to continue alone, developing the specific aspects of our dream.

My passion for research led me to become a writer, researcher, speaker and developer of methods of personal growth. Edgar's passion for magic led him to become a modern day shaman, within the western world.

Ten years later I met Edgar again, incarnating the dream that has motivated him ever since he was a boy: I found him a shaman with apprentices from all over the world. And in spite of all the success that he has had in his task, I can still see the spirit of the adventurous boy that has enormous fun and maintains his simplicity, even in the midst of the most demanding battles.

His book opens the door for all those who are curious about having a first encounter with the joy of his shamanic world.

Víctor Sánchez is the author of 'The Teachings of Don Carlos - Practical Applications of the Works of Carlos Castaneda' and 'The Toltec Path of Recapitulation'.

AUTHOR'S PREFACE

It is my desire to sow a seed of consciousness. I hope that as my readers meet my particular beliefs about knowledge, they will realise that they are just one more way of understanding reality.

When I started writing this book I thought that I was doing it for myself; now I see that I am only a channel for Spirit, so that this knowledge can be spread in a poetic way.

I haven't written the book in a linear way and I don't expect it to be read in a linear way. A large part of what I offer here has been adapted so that it will be understandable to those people who haven't been my apprentices; for those who have worked with me it is a good way of recovering those long conversations that we have had, as well as a beautiful memento of the marvellous moments we have shared.

I'm not trying to say that everything that appears here happened exactly as I have written. That wouldn't be true, just as it wouldn't be true to say that it is the fruit of my imagination. For me, this book is like a legend, a myth; half real and half fantasy, transfigured by my own interpretation of events and by the need to write something that would be a payment for everything that I have read and that has enlarged my soul.

As I read what I have written, I recognize the influence of José, of my family, of the Nagual, of Mariví and of Victor, all of them shamans. I'd like to make it clear that I have taken their concepts, modifying them to my own beliefs and experiences. I have reused their words because they were the ones they used with me; they are my memories. I give thanks for their devastating influence on my apprentice soul and for all the confusion that it implies: I no longer know when I am thinking, or when I am thinking what they were thinking. Nor do I know if I am writing or if it is their consensus in my soul that dictates the words.

Be that as it may, thank you.

There are three souls in my soul:
Mine, yours and God's.
The consensus of the three is called love,
Which is the energy that unites the universe
And is manifested in service and in happiness,
Creating a harmonious cloud around us.

Nothing disturbs this harmony.
There is no disharmony.
Internal peace sowed its seed
And the souls became one.

Everything begins when consciousness awakens
And follows the path of the stars.
Life takes shape
Creating a myth where none existed.
Creating a dream in nothingness.

From the second book of *Memories Stolen from the Dead Stars*

BOOK ONE

THE GARDEN
OF KNOWLEDGE

In a place near the sacred mountains of the Catalonian Pyrenees, a young Mexican shaman stopped his wanderings, tired of his travels through the world. He had found a large farmhouse and had recognized that the place was a sacred site from earlier times. Celts and Christians had built their sanctuaries there, and the mountains overflowed with magic and freedom. He felt the prophecies of his ancestors coming nearer with the passing of each day, and that this was the most important place of his life. Here was where he would die so that he could be reborn. This was the place where he would fulfil his destiny. So he settled down and prepared himself, waiting for omens and signs from the Great Spirit.

Contradictory feelings marked this evolutionary stage. His soul, in its process of transformation, had split into two. Everything was contradictory, yet immersed in a phantom balance. He felt a lot of love as well as great unconcern for all those who surrounded him; he felt great sadness, but he was happy all day; he felt great fury but also internal peace; great emptiness in his soul, although he had never been so completely full, and he felt great tiredness, but also unusual strength. Everything in him was contradictory. He was unknown to himself; or better said, two unknowns.

In his confusion his only guide was his shamanic code, his code of impeccability.

He felt confused and lost. He knew what he wanted and

what he didn't want. But he didn't know how to achieve his objectives.

While trying to understand the prophecies of his life and what Spirit wanted from him, he dug a small tomb and turned it into his dwelling. Giving it a roof and an altar, he transformed it into his bedroom. It was a burrow in the shape of a cross, some five square metres in size, and a metre high – "A womb," he said, "where my beloved Mother Earth will allow me to heal my split soul."

Every night, after carrying out his sacred movements, a sort of dance based on what are known as 'magical passes', he said goodnight to the people of the house, and went to sleep in his tomb. He felt lost in the sea of consciousness, with no fixed direction, not knowing what was the next step Spirit would signal to him. Only his shamanic code kept him at the tireless work of those who are seekers of knowledge.

Sadness showed in his face when he remembered how everything that he had struggled to achieve for ten years had fallen apart. So much searching for the Sacred Shaman of Los Angeles, so much effort to join the group of the Nagual, so that finally one afternoon the Nagual could approach him and say in a paternal tone:

"I have to tell you personally··· this is not your place."

MEMORIES OF THE NAGUAL

Lluisa, who lived in the farmhouse, approached the shaman one day. Looking up at the sky, he felt he wanted to pour out all that he had in his soul. He decided to explain the reason for his withdrawal into his womb of Earth, and so he recalled that warm afternoon in Los Angeles.

"For a couple of hours the Nagual's helpers had been checking each of us in the room, looking for something. I didn't understand and the situation scared me. Finally the Nagual Woman looked at the sole of my foot. I had a mark on it, like the footprint of a bear.

'Here it is!' she cried, calling the attention of everyone in the room.

Everyone came over to look at the mark. Fear invaded

me. Finally the Nagual arrived and, without looking me in the eyes, in a paternal voice, he told me:

'I have to tell you personally: this is not your place.'

The need to cry like a little child swamped my shaman's apprentice soul. My sobs were stronger than my warrior's desire to control myself. I didn't understand the words, but their meaning was clear. I cried like a child; it was the first and only time that the Nagual embraced me.

'I am your Nagual, but this is not your place. This is the place of the green apprentices and you are blue,' he told me. In this way I learnt the name of my lineage. 'I simply give you your freedom. You are free.'

With these words my destiny was set."

Lluisa saw how the young man cried inside as he recounted his memories. And she saw how he tried to make the most out of the situation.

"'What does Spirit want of me?' I asked myself again and again. 'What does it mean to be blue? Why did I struggle so much to reach a place that wasn't mine in the end?'

I wasn't interested in the freedom that I had fought for. I only wanted to be there with them, with him. I wanted to listen to him and follow his instructions blindly. My whole life struggling to reach that place, with those people, to find out, in the end, that it wasn't for me. I didn't want a freedom that I didn't understand. I only wanted to be there and feel the love of that marvellous man.

A free man cannot be the slave of a free teacher. I wanted to be his slave, and he wouldn't allow it.

'Now what shall I do with my freedom?' I asked myself again and again, whilst I gazed at the cultivated fields of those mountains of the Catalonian Pyrenees.

'Be congruent with your knowledge' was the answer that my mind always offered. Only sleeping within the Earth gives me sobriety and joy."

"Agustín, don't you think you are hiding?" Inma asked him.

"The freedom that I have earned through my own efforts allows me to hide if I want, but, wherever I am, my karma or destiny will come for me. I can't escape Spirit, or consciousness, just as I can't escape the power that rules my life.

I have to understand and be congruent with my knowledge; I am not interested in confrontation. I am only interested in evolving and I need energy from Mother Earth to access all my resources and carry on.

I have lost the dream that I struggled for all my life. I know that Spirit doesn't take anything away without giving something better in return. For this reason Spirit, in love, has placed me beneath your protective shadow, Inma. No one can ever hide from Spirit."

The news spread that in this farmhouse, called 'La Plana', far from any town or city, sleeping in a hole in the ground, there was a shaman who had the ability to see energy directly and interpret it. This brought curious people and apprentices of shamanism to the sacred grounds. In time, the place began to become famous, mainly because of the friendliness of the owner, Inma, as well as that of the other people who lived there: Concha, Albert, Armand and the rest of the helpers. Inma, an old soul in service to humanity, was very attentive to the shaman and all those that reached her territory. The young shaman, Agustín, saw Inma as a queen.

Every day new people arrived looking for his advice and his words. They knew that the shaman saw reality from a different point.

"I am tired of talking", he explained one day to a group of people who had come to learn from him, "but it is one of the tasks that I was born to. Spirit has taught me according to the law of the sacred word. I have the obligation and the pleasure of sharing my interpretation of life, but you must understand that it is my interpretation; it is my way of constructing my harmonious reality within the designs of Spirit. It is only a personal interpretation of how I believe reality to be."

"I'll teach you, and you can help me to carry stones," he continued. "We'll make a bargain: knowledge in exchange for what I need and you are in a position to offer."

In this way they began to organize and formalize their meetings. Agustín and the people who approached him built sanctuaries within the Earth, and 'nests' in the treetops, amongst other facilities that the shaman considered appropriate to his work, and they held long conversations about any subject that arose, from the most mundane to the most magical, according to the atmosphere created in each situation.

"Agustín, how did you learn to dream?" asked Carmen Yoldi.

"It was amongst shamans in Oaxaca, with María Sabina, who is a very good friend of José, my benefactor. He took me to Huautla so that she could teach me.

María Sabina

I was in a tiny village in the mountains of Oaxaca. I was still looking for the right way to live and Spirit again placed me before a woman shaman to teach me.

"You must eat the little mushrooms," her daughter translated, "let 'the children' talk to you."

María only spoke Mazateco, and one of her daughters translated some of her words from time to time.

"I am scared María, I can't get the idea out if my head that they're drugs," I answered.

"The little mushrooms aren't drugs," the woman shaman assured me, translated by her daughter. "They are plants of Power, the flesh of the gods; they are the children of the woods that speak to us."

"I only want to find the right way to live, the right way to walk through life," I emphasized to explain my objection to taking what, in my ignorance, I considered to be exclusively a hallucinogen.

Then María began to talk in Mazateco and didn't stop until some two hours had passed, during which time I couldn't take my eyes or my attention off her in spite of understanding absolutely nothing that she said.

"Take this plant before sleeping," she said on finishing her monologue, "it's called San Pedro."

"OK" I answered, whilst looking at the dry crumbs of what had been a green leaf. I went to my hut, placed a pinch of the herb under my tongue as she had indicated, and went to bed. Before falling asleep I had a strange feeling of dizziness.

In the middle of the night I woke up and got up suddenly. Someone had pulled me by the elbow and I saw María standing before me.

21

"María, what are you doing here? Can I help you with anything?" I asked in surprise, with complete innocence.

"I've come to teach you how to find the right way to live. One only learns in dreams and one only earns in life."

"María, I can understand everything you say. Can you speak Spanish now?"

"The children, the plants, have brought me to your dream. Right now you are dreaming."

"Oh⋯" I said, without understanding the implications of what she had said, "⋯but⋯ how did you learn Spanish so fast?"

"Languages don't exist in dreams. Look at yourself there asleep."

I looked at my bed and I saw myself there curled up in a ball. I felt the impact in my stomach and I wanted to wake myself up, but María wouldn't let me. She took me gently by the hand and we went off to walk in the woods, where we talked at length about her knowledge.

Hours later I awoke in my hut with a drunken feeling that lasted until I fell back off to sleep. Then I dreamt that I spoke with another Indian and I awoke again, this time wide-awake and lucid.

I discovered from my experience of that night that the plant San Pedro had hallucinogenic effects, and as I thought that each dream was simply a hallucination, I didn't give importance to the knowledge the dreams offered.

From then onwards, each night someone came to talk to me, but now without me taking San Pedro, and in the end I never agreed to take the mushrooms. Almost always, in my dreams, someone took me walking to a cave somewhere in the area and the following morning I easily found each new place that had been shown to me during the night.

One night I awoke in my bedroll, everything was spinning around and I felt myself slipping into a state of hallucination. I fell asleep again and I noticed a strong hand taking me by the neck. I tried to move but wasn't able to; I tried to scream but couldn't. I had my eyes open and a voice whispered in my ear 'compose yourself'. My fear grew and I had to make an effort to avoid waking up. The presence lifted me up in the air and, after getting my energetic body out of my physical body, raised me higher until I was floating in the room, looking at my body laid down. Then the presence took me through the woods as if pushing me on a stretcher trolley, which terrified me.

We reached a cave. The presence placed me in an upright position and I immediately recovered my mobility. Facing me I found another of the Indians from the village. He was small and chubby and he had a wide smile.

"I'm going to take you to a cavern, and there you will make your warrior's promise" he said.

We were in the depths of a large cave. An immense circular cavern rose majestically above our heads. Facing us hung a stalactite that shone in a colour somewhere between gold and peach, guarded by two electric blue columns, one on each side, like guardians of its beauty. I understood that the hanging stone was the warrior and that the cavern represented a doorway into other worlds. The stalactite began to breathe, or to do something that I interpreted as inhaling and exhaling, and I waited for it to say something to me.

" Don't worry about whether it will address you," said the Indian. "This warrior has existed since before humanity. Make your offering and, if your words have power, he will listen to them. If your life is upright, he will look for you one day when you need him and he will remind you of your words. But be careful about what you say because you must fulfil your promise. This is not like a promise from the western world that you can squander in the future."

I was scared. Something in me understood the importance of this meeting. I took a couple of hours to make my promise and my offering to power, and I awoke again, feeling drunk in my room.

It took me close to ten years to find that cavern in the real world. I knew its name: Cacahuamilpa. Only then could I remember my offering and my warrior's pact.

THE ARK

The entire universe converges on one point.
Each place is linked to All through threads of light.
There are worlds and anti-worlds,
Men and anti-men:
They converge at the same point in parallel universes.

From the second book of *Memories Stolen from the Dead Stars*

Except for that one time, when I had to wait ten years to confirm the existence of the place in my dream, every morning I found the place where I had been taken in my last dreaming experience.

On another occasion, I awoke at five in the morning. The full moon rested on a sea of clouds in the distance and the mountain over my hut seemed to have reached the sky, and even gone beyond it. I heard a voice. "Agustín," it said clearly. I found myself standing facing an Indian with a radiating smile. He was different to those I had seen so far in my life. He was very dark, very strong, and with a sculptural body. He was wearing a simple loincloth, sandals knotted up to his knees, and a white band held his long dark hair in place.

"Come with me," he said. It was midday and we set off walking from the village, where nobody appeared to be surprised by his appearance. I greeted various people I knew but none of them replied. We travelled from there to the city of Oaxaca in a bus, remaining on foot for almost the entire journey, while the Indian asked me about the characteristics of my life, my routines and my feelings.

From Oaxaca we took another bus that went in the direction of the mountains and we alighted in the middle of a forest.

"Pay close attention to how to get here," the Indian said, pointing out a track. "This path will take you to my hamlet." It surprised me that he said 'hamlet' rather than 'village'. I observed a very beautiful tree, strange and ancient. The tree sheltered me and at that moment I understood that I was in a dream, from which I awoke in my room when it was almost night.

I went to eat in the same place as I did every night and the Indian woman that served me was interested in where I had been all day. I told her that I had been sleeping.

The next morning, very early, I got my rucksack, my sleeping bag and the provisions I had in my room, and I left the village without saying goodbye to anyone. My only intention was to confirm my nocturnal route and I planned to return to Huautla, but I never did. I never said goodbye to María. I never thanked her nor paid her anything for her knowledge and her attentions.

Everything was exactly as I had dreamed it, except that when I got off the bus I was accompanied by a young man, also a sorcerer's apprentice called Antonio. He told me that he had spent two years looking for one of the Arks of Humanity. Of course I wrote him off as crazy, but his company was pleasant and I found his camping equipment interesting because it all seemed to indicate that the road would be a long one.

"What's all this about an ark?" I asked him, while poking the fire that we had lit in the camp we had set up for the night. He was from Mexico City, a 'white' with fine features, and no trace of an Indian ancestry. He had a thick chestnut beard and was slightly robust.

"One day I dreamed that there were three arks in the world," he explained. "One in the Gobi desert, another in Africa, and another in the mountains of Oaxaca."

"Three arks! Like Noah's?" I asked with interest.

"I'm not sure. I only know that I have to look for one, but I've already lost any hope that I will find it. Maybe it was only a dream⋯."

"A dream brought me here too," I told him, and recounted the story.

"Very interesting," he said, "perhaps it's no coincidence that we have met and that I decided to get off the bus with you in the middle of these mountains."

The mountains of Oaxaca are a jewel among jewels, beautiful both for the people who live there and the whispers and sighs of the Earth: it is possible to walk among the clouds there, and even above them.

A sudden noise brought Antonio to his feet from the mat

where he had been lying.

"Did you hear that?" he asked.

"No. What is it?" I said in fright. I was afraid that someone might want to rob us, or that it was one of the bears that
inhabited the region.

"Listen," he said in a whisper.

Around us could be heard the sound of branches breaking,
and I was afraid. I saw shadows behind the trees that moved
at great speed, but I thought that it was my imagination, and I
seemed to hear a growl.

"I think we are surrounded by a herd of pumas," I said.

"Pumas don't move in herds," he reassured me.

The atmosphere had changed and we began to hear
breathing. Antonio was terrified. My deafness meant I could
hardly hear it, but I felt the pressure of the breathing around
us. It was like being in a paper bag that someone was breathing in and out of.

"I'm sure it's a bear," he told me, "But the breathing
seems to come from everywhere."

My deafness gave me certain advantages. I was made
more afraid by Antonio's fear than by the small noises that I
could hear, or the physical sensations I perceived.

A couple of hours passed with no change. Antonio was on
the edge of collapse, while unconsciously I was hearing less
and less. A part of me knew how to disconnect from the
noises and become almost totally deaf. So, embolden by my
deafness, with the certainty that it couldn't be bandits because they would already have attacked us, and bored now by
Antonio's terror, I asked him for the machete he held tightly in
his hands. I gave him my torch so that he could give me light
while I picked up a stone with the intention of throwing it at
whatever was terrorizing us.

"Where is the breathing coming from?" I asked him.

Without speaking a word Antonio pointed with difficulty at
some bushes. I advanced decidedly in spite of Antonio asking
me not to, until I was two metres from the spot that Antonio
had indicated. I screamed at the same time as I threw the rock
with all my strength, and something the size of a hare ran from
out of the bushes. I laughed out loud.

"That little animal has had us terrified for hours," I said between laughs.

Antonio laughed with me. His laugh was nervous and he tried to become infected by my joy, but he was pale.

Unconcerned and joking I suggested we break camp, and we set off along the path in the middle of the night.

Two hours later we set up camp again.

"Agustín, you are really brave," Antonio told me, now calmer.

"Thanks," I said with pride.

"How could you laugh in the face of that enormous thing?"

"What? That little animal?"

"No. An enormous shadow came out from behind the animal. It began to growl louder and the sound of the breathing became noisier and it was a metre above your head. It seemed like the more you laughed the angrier it got. The only reason I didn't run off was because you were so calm and happy."

I felt atrocious fear. Seeing the little creature had made me laugh and it hadn't occurred to me to look to see if there was anything else in the bushes. I had paid no attention to any sounds other than my voice and my laughter. The type of deafness I suffer from prevents me from hearing more than one thing at a time. If I laugh I can't hear anything else. I fell to the floor and thought that my bowels would empty right there. I ended up vomiting from sheer nerves.

I tried to explain my hearing problem to Antonio, but it was impossible because I was suddenly very tired. I got into my sleeping bag, thanking my deafness, but because of my nervousness I couldn't get off to sleep until the sun came up. A strange early morning fog wrapped itself around us.

THE HAMLET
OF THE ANCIENT MEXICANS

"Agustín, wake up! Quick, wake up!" Antonio said.

"What's up?" I woke up reluctantly, regretting travelling with a companion. "What's up?" I repeated.

"Look," said Antonio, pointing around us.

We were on a plain, like a steppe, totally flat and treeless. In the distance mountains could be seen, as if we were in the centre of a valley.

"What about it?" I asked bad-temperedly. I was tired and I didn't like being woken up roughly.

"This isn't the same place we went to sleep in last night."

"What?" I said in surprise.

He was right. We had camped close to some trees. I remembered it well because when I had lain down and tried to see the stars in the sky, I couldn't because the branches were in the way. Now we weren't even on a path. I remembered perfectly the night time hike, because I had been the guide, and now there were neither mountains nor ravines.

"Perhaps we are dreaming," I said.

"No, this isn't a dream," he replied with certainty.

My way of telling whether I was experiencing a dream or not was to try to remember what I had done the day before. If I managed it and it was a linear sequence of events, then I knew I was in the world of everyday physical reality. In dreams it was impossible to achieve this type of remembering because time works in a different way. I thought about everything I had done the day before and it was all linear, I remembered everything perfectly: this couldn't be a dream.

"Agustín, look," said Antonio, bringing me back from my thoughts, pointing at something again.

Four Indians were walking towards us with long, calm steps. They were wearing blankets tied at the shoulder and white loincloths, their long hair was tied up with a headband and they were wearing neither jewellery nor paint. They looked like actors from a film about the Pre-Hispanic world.

"Kuali tonali," they said, offering a white smile.

"Kuali," I answered, recognizing the Nahuatl greeting, which made me think that they were from a village in the Norte de Puebla Mountains.

"Where are we?" I asked, more confident now I believed I had recognized them.

"You're here!" they said, laughing.

"We're a little lost. Could you tell us where the nearest village is?" I asked, trying to start a conversation.

"You bet you're lost!" said the tallest, darkest man, as again they all laughed like little children.

"But how did you manage to cross the doorway?" asked one of the Indians with white hair, while the others laughed again. Their laughter began to make me nervous.

"Could you take us to your village or wherever you are going? We're hungry and we'll pay for our food." I wanted to tempt them with money so that they would be more communicative and respectful.

They didn't answer. They just burst out laughing again. I began to think they were drunk.

"Are we inside an ark?" asked Antonio shyly.

"That's right, young friend," he answered. "Somehow you managed to cross the doorway and avoid the guardian."

I felt more shame than fear.

"How did you get through the door?" asked the oldest.

"It was him," said Antonio, pointing at me shyly.

The Indians burst out laughing again. I felt ridiculous and out of place. I couldn't understand what was going on.

"Don't blush," said the old man who introduced himself as Coatl, which means snake.

"I am Acatl Caña," said the tallest man, "and these are Meztli and Toztli," he added, pointing to the other two, who had remained silent. His good Spanish surprised me. I told him and they all laughed again.

"Kuatli," said one of them, and that was when I noticed that they didn't move their mouths. They hadn't spoken a single word in the entire conversation. We were communicating in some telepathic way. I felt my knees giving way and I leant on Antonio, who was in no better condition. We had crossed a doorway into another world or another epoch.

We suddenly found ourselves in a village built of adobe bricks and canes, where we were invited into one of the houses, and left alone there. It was very clean and comfortable, full of well-arranged furniture, which gave it a feeling of order and convenience. Everything was very rustic and very beautiful. Antonio and I, left alone, talked about our impressions.

What's going on?" I asked him.

"It looks like that presence yesterday was the guardian of the door, and destiny decreed that you would be deaf and that I would find you. This enabled us to defeat the guardian and cross through."

"I don't feel as though I've defeated anybody, and I don't remember any doorway."

"Don't be stupid!" Antonio reproached me. "Look around you: none of this belongs to our social order." He was right.

At that point seven old men and seven youths entered, introducing themselves respectively as the seven underworlds and the seven paradises. They spoke with us, mainly with Antonio, and they decided to separate us. Nothing had frightened me more in any of my earlier experiences.

"What am I doing here?" I asked Acatl.

"That is a mystery Agustín. Very few people pass from your world to my world."

"Who are you?" I inquired.

"We are ancient inhabitants of the valley of Anahuac and we were trapped in a bubble of time in the epoch of the arrival of the whites," explained Acatl.

"But that was 500 years ago!" I exclaimed.

"My grandfather, who is now dead, was a priest and a shaman and, in order to save the village, he put us into this parallel world."

"What are parallel worlds?" I wanted to know.

"It's as if three spheres or more occupied the same space, and very seldom do they meet up, perhaps once every 100 years, and even then it is very difficult for someone to pass from one to another of them. I have never seen anyone from the other world close up."

"And why am I here?" I insisted, worriedly.

"Definitely to help Antonio cross the doorway. He would never have managed it alone."

They let me move freely around the hamlet, which was an exact reproduction of what I had always imagined a village from before the time of the Spanish conquest to be like. There were three pyramids with their temples, surrounded by an innumerable number of huts and small palaces, and all the houses were whitewashed and had gardens on the roof terraces.

One day they invited me on a hunt. Their telepathic communication made them very effective at hunting, and their cookery was truly exquisite. I enjoyed their dishes so much that I even began to believe that that was my reason for being in the village, as it seemed that the only thing I did was to wait for mealtimes!

They spoke with me about many things that I couldn't understand, but they told me that a part of my consciousness would one day reach understanding. During the day they hardly spoke to me, but at night time they always approached, above all when I was asleep.

Every hour they came to wake me up and ask me to jump, and then they marked the distance on the floor. It was always one of the seven old men from the underworld who came, and shook me by the elbow. I got up and jumped as far as I could. It went on like that every night until I noticed that Antonio came with them. My jumps got longer and longer, until one day I realized that I was jumping seven metres. This surprised me, but everything was so strange that it didn't bother me. A few more nights like that went by, until I asked the old man what was going on. In reply he pointed to my bed and once more I saw myself there, lying down. "I've taken that San Pedro herb again," I thought.

Through the door came the first Indian that I had seen, who had shown me how to reach the path that led to the village, from the middle of the forest.

"Hello," I said, and a part of me understood everything.

"I am speaking with your Yogual, your energetic body, your dreaming body, your astral body."

It seemed that I had to confirm that I understood, so I nodded.

"We won't have time to teach you to do it voluntarily, as we have with Antonio"

I felt that I was missing something.

"But now it is formed and shaped," he continued, "you have survived your first entrance into other worlds, and in the future you will have to do it alone."

While he spoke I understood that it would be the last time

that I would see him.

"The first time that our ancestors jumped into this world," he explained, "you should have come with us, you should have stayed within this ark of protection, but you decided to continue your journey, reaching out to your people who couldn't pass into this world and so were trapped in the world of normal life."

I was overcome by great sadness.

"Once," he said, "there was a child who woke up crying. His mother consoled him as the child explained his nightmare: he and one of his brothers were carrying a sack full of colourful seeds, some red beans. The sack tore open and the little red beans were spread out all over the world, in the most unsuspected places. The child cried because he knew that his task was to find every single one of these seeds. It seemed an impossible task⋯"

I knew that the Indian was talking about the dreams that I had had as a child.

"You still have to face two confrontations, and both of them will be in your Yogual, Agustín," he announced.

I embraced him. Something in me could remember him, but it wasn't my normal consciousness. My energetic body entered into my physical body, and I woke up. Around me were the people of the village. The Indian, whose name I never knew, was at the head of the crowd with my luggage in his hands. Antonio was standing next to him with his own luggage on his back. I embraced the Indian whilst holding back my tears. After saying goodbye to each of them, I picked up my things and began to walk with Antonio, until it got dark ten hours later.

We set up camp, eating none of the food they had given us, and we hardly spoke a word. We went to bed, and on awakening the following morning, saw that the landscape had changed again. We found ourselves in another region of Oaxaca a month later. That was where I said goodbye to Antonio.

"It will be very difficult for us to meet again," he told me. "Only if we have an objective in common will Spirit bring us together."

I have never seen him since.

I didn't see him again there, nor in any of the other places I have travelled through. Not even in a dream. I don't know where or when he or the rest of those people existed. But now I know how to dream reality, and I know that I can jump as far as I want, and I know that you don't have to talk to communicate, and I know that when I see a red seed scatte-red – a poem, a person, or simply a smile – I must gather it··· just in case everything that I experienced was only a memory that I stole from a dead star believing that it still existed.

The truly wise aren't wise.
The truly wise don't know that they are wise.
There is no true seer in existence that declares himself to be a
seer,
Yet all his being knows that he is.

From the second book of *Memories Stolen from the Dead Stars*

CONVERSATIONS
IN THE GARDEN OF KNOWLEDGE

"Speak to us about Spirit," said a young doctor called José María.

"It takes an entire life to clean our relationship with Spirit. Spirit or the Great Spirit is everything that exists, has existed or will exist. It is the Great Consciousness, creator of the Cosmos. We can't understand it, it is too big and mysterious, but we can witness it, we can understand its commands, we can try to decipher its harmonious whims. We can enter into it; travel in its mysteries.

We can handle the energy if we are in harmony with it.

Spirit has compassion for no one, feels pity for no one; it only obeys harmony and your personal power. Spirit doesn't guess what you want, it obeys what you know how to request from it. You need humility, clarity, a lot of energy and the capacity to direct this energy to one single place in order to give Spirit a command.

Spirit is the great consciousness and we are one of its manifestations: small and limited, but exquisite manifestations of consciousness."

"Speak to us about shamanism," requested Ken, a Norwegian homeopath.

"The shaman is an intermediary between this incompre-

34

hensible energy and the people that surround him. The shaman is a magical being that tries to untangle the mysteries of life. He is a lover of knowledge and the mystery. The shaman is poet and visionary.

In shamanism there are two currents that, like two snakes, interlace. One is that of the healer, and the other, that of the sacred word. Both are united in service to humanity, in love for this world, and in the journey through the unknown.

Our shamanic lineage has its roots in the effort to fall in love with this world, to love life, to love knowledge, to love oneself as a human being···"

"How did you know you were a shaman?" asked Jorge, who lived in Cadiz.

"I must have been 25 when I had the following dream:

In front of my bed I saw the messenger of death. He manifested as a skeleton with a black cape. I could only see his hands and his skull, which glowed with an amber light.

When I saw him I was very angry. For many years I had been a potential suicide with a great desire to die and to leave this world. I couldn't see any meaning to life and I couldn't see a single reason to live.

I looked at the messenger of death and I said to him:

'For many years I wanted to die, I was dying because I couldn't die, I called you and you didn't come for me, but today I can't go with you. Finally I like life, finally I have found a reason to live.'

The messenger of death looked me in the eyes and said:

'I only came so that you would know.'

The messenger of death is a presence that has always been with me, both in my apprenticeship, and in the teaching that I am now doing.

The next day I told José, my benefactor and teacher, about my dream, and he simply said:

'Agustín, you are now a shaman. Finally you have fallen in love with life.'

One week later I had opened my office as an energetic therapist."

"If I make an effort on the shamanic path, Agustín, will I be able to avoid reincarnating in this world?" asked Maricarmen.

"I'll tell you a story so that you can understand what shamanism is. Once upon a time there was a pilgrim who was going to the cave of a holy shaman. He wanted to ask him how many incarnations he still needed to experience to reach illumination and avoid having to be reborn into this world.

On his way to the cave he met a farmer who was looking at the field that he was planning to plough.

'Hey, farmer!' he called out, 'Do you want me to ask the holy shaman how many lives you need to live to reach illumination and so not have to come back to this world?'

'OK,' agreed the man, as he contemplated the clouds and the mountains.

The pilgrim continued walking until he met a yogi who was meditating by a waterfall.

'Hey, yogi!' he shouted.

'Don't disturb me, I'm chanting my mantras,' answered the yogi in irritation.

'I'm sorry. I thought you'd want me to ask the holy shaman how many lives you have left before you reach illumination.'

'Of course, please do, I'm working hard to make this my last life in this world, and I'd be grateful if you'd ask.'

The pilgrim visited the shaman and on his return the anxious yogi was waiting for him between mantras.

'How many lives have I got left?' asked the yogi, nervously.

'The holy shaman said two.'

'What? How many? I'm going to work harder to see if I can manage it in one. Excuse me; I'm going to chant my mantras. Om mane padme hum, Om mane padme hum, Om mane padme hum, Om mane padme hum, Two lives! What a pity! Om mane padme hum···'

The pilgrim continued on his way, listening to the yogi's mantras. A little later he met the farmer working the land.

'Hey, farmer!'

'Yes?'

36

'I asked the holy shaman.'
'Ah! How many lives have I got left?'
'Three hundred and sixty-five.'
'Three hundred and sixty-five?'
'That's what he said.'
'Great! When life is so beautiful···'
And in that moment the farmer reached illumination."

Agustín had another name, his Indian name, Ce Acatl Itzcoatl Papalotzin. He was a wise man, sad and worldly. His rustic, wild world contrasted with his urban way of life. While in his burrow his behaviour was that of a man who enjoyed living in nature, who liked to spend long hours contemplating the wild boar of the area; when he had to go to the city to sell his handicrafts, he wore his best suit. Agustín was half wild and half urban, and he moved between these two poles with great harmony.

He had no material goods, yet he never lacked for anything. The people of La Plana were surprised by his ability to get whatever he was looking for.

"Speak to us about money," said a young woman from Wales called Sophia, who was a healer who often had problems with money and was trying to resolve them.

Agustín climbed onto a large stone and said:

"The shaman knows that he shouldn't worry about material things, but neither should he reject them. The shaman isn't at war with money, and he always has a strategy for how to deal with his economic order. When the apprentice doesn't have a strategy, he lets Spirit take charge of him, and then he is obedient before any manifestation of Spirit.

The shaman takes responsibility for saving energy. He knows that the material world is moved with the energy of the little finger, but he also knows that it takes a lot of energy to be an apprentice. The shaman has a pact with Spirit: Spirit looks after his interests, and he looks after the interests of Spirit.

The shaman knows that Spirit doesn't accept requests or demands; Spirit only obeys personal power, and this personal power is stored in the belly area, in the centre of energy. When the shaman sends an order, conjuration or respectful indication to Spirit, he knows that his request is conditioned by the amount of personal power that he has available and that corresponds to him through his karma.

The shaman doesn't invoke rubbish, but he doesn't deny himself anything either. If the shaman takes the path of abstinence and poverty, he is responsible for his own decision; for this reason he neither regrets nor complains. The shaman knows that he lives in an abundant Universe, and that this abundance is at his disposal. He only needs to know how to invoke it from his absolute certainty.

Every time he receives money, he offers it symbolically to Spirit, taking it to first to his forehead and then offering it to the sky, making a mental or verbal invocation: 'This money will return to you 100 times.' And every time that he gives money he makes the following invocation: 'The money that leaves my left hand, will return to my right hand 100 times.' He never counts money, he makes a roll of it and he puts it in his pocket, knowing that it will reproduce by itself.

He never feels compassion when charging or paying; he knows how to value his personal work. He never asks for charity for his work, but he is flexible with people in need, and his flexibility is a way of thanking Spirit.

Money is energy. Green energy. One cannot be a first-rate spiritual man and a second-rate material man. The shaman tries to balance magic with the everyday world. He doesn't fight against the social order. He doesn't fight against money. He doesn't fight against material goods, or against those who live in abundance.

Spiritual people justify their lack through spirituality, with beliefs of the type 'I'm not rich but I will enter into the kingdom of Heaven⋯' In their supposed attempt to stop being slaves to money, they become slaves to spirituality.

Look at me; I am a slave to neither money nor spirituality. Cleaning my links to money doesn't make me a slave to money. Until I was thirty I lived a vow of poverty. Now my pact with God is one of abundance and economic solvency and I will never again lack for anything because I have agreed this with Spirit.

Money is there to serve consciousness, and not the other way round. Consciousness cannot put itself at the service of money.

We live in an abundant Universe. Why should you feel limited? Why should you be at a disadvantage? Where are your promises of poverty, your feelings of guilt towards money, and your incapacity to value your work as an artist? Look at Freda. She is proud of her paintings and her art, but when she tries to sell she puts her work on the table apologetically and says: 'That's a thousand dollars, but I'll let you have it for eight hundred and I won't accept less than five hundred···' In three seconds she has demeaned herself before money. She doesn't feel she can charge what her work is really worth.

Why don't you know how to value yourself in this life? Whether you like it or not, you are a dealer in knowledge and a dealer in healing. When you give a therapy you charge but you feel like you are burning your hands. Offer this money to Spirit and dedicate yourself to service. Take what you deserve without taking anything away from anyone. Learn to give and learn to receive. If you charge, do it well. You have to repeat over and over again: 'I want to, I can, I deserve to.'

Sophia went off with her head down to revise the promises she had made in the past. She knew that she had to change her way of thinking and that this task would require all her attention and effort. She was tired of feeling poor and of having problems with money.

One day Juan, one of the most veteran and marvellous apprentices of all, arrived. He had led a simple, disciplined life. The Nagual's Group had freed him, like Agustín, so that he could grow straight or twisted, and full of energy and personal power, he had realized that the only thing he had in the world was his life of discipline. He had decided to use his energy to get a wife and to have money.

Esperanza, who didn't understand what had happened to Juan, who had been an example for all to follow, asked in disappointment: "Agustín, talk to us about greed."

"Greed is one of the natural enemies of the apprentice.

You covet what you don't have and would like to have, what seems very distant, and you look for an easy way to get it. It's right there that the dark side of reality hangs over you, stalks you, and when you least expect it, offers you an opportunity, but in some way that you consider inappropriate. Then you don't know whether to break your pacts with Spirit and take advantage of the opportunity, or to let it go.

Greed is disguised as a good opportunity. '···You can earn a lot of money with very little work···' Ask yourself, and only yourself, if you will regret it, if this opportunity will harm your fellow creatures, or if it will give you the feeling of abusing anyone or stealing. If you know you are going to regret it, leave it. If not, take responsibility for the consequences.

We covet what others have because we don't have it. Wanting to be or have something is wonderful, but the dark side stalks us, waiting for us to make a mistake in our pacts with God.

Juan has failed in everything but he has triumphed in life. If his choice is free of the dark side of reality, then he will triumph in the end. For him it is extremely important to triumph and to move upwards socially, economically and in consciousness. Ambition is a good thing, as long as it doesn't trap you in the dark side of reality. He is caught in the con‒tradiction of ambition. He is at a 'sandwich' point: he is neither a common man, nor a social triumph.

One should aspire to more, always to more, but without getting trapped in greed. You must respect your pacts with Spirit and work."

One winter morning two of Agustín's best apprentices arrived: a man and a woman, Pablo and Karola, two tireless travellers, and great searchers after knowledge. They were facing their destiny, but doubt was eating them up.

By the fire in the tipi that they had put up in the middle of the woods that surrounded the house, after two hours of silence, Agustín broke the sacred to manifest the worldly:

"I have travelled through so many places," he said without lifting his eyes from the fire, "···so many countries in search of knowledge···.I have spoken with teachers, seers, prophets, and even with politicians to find out why I am in this world," he added, while he thought of the tomb where he would sleep that night.

Silence invaded the countryside.

Karola, who was a charming woman and a great conversationalist, broke the silence trying to begin a conversation. Her desire to talk showed in her eyes.

"Speak to us of knowledge – she asked with great joy.

"You want me to talk to you about knowledge, Karolita, but your questions only lead me to talk about what I know and you to talk about what you know. We learn new ways to play with words, but knowledge is more than words. Words are puffs of air that leave your mouth harmoniously. Knowledge is the congruence with which we tie up all our acts.

If you really want to know, listen; don't speak. But don't listen to me; don't listen to an intermediary, look for the source yourself. Listen to Mother Earth, the Mother Creator of the Universe.

Look, Karolita, you have great wisdom and your way of life provides the framework; knowledge courts you but sometimes you lose everything through your lack of internal or external silence. Nobody has given you anything. Everything you have in your life you have earned through your own merit. I have never seen you complain, except on rare occasions, nor criticize with malice. God, Spirit, loves you, for what you are and for what you have allowed yourself to be. Your life has not been easy. You are a fighter, a woman of courage and spirit.

Silence inundated the tipi. Pablo had perceived the message as if it was directed at him and he looked at Agustín. He wanted to speak, but he didn't dare to break the sacred silence. Agustín nodded his head and Pablo let out the confusion of his soul.

"I feel defeated and I haven't even begun. I play with words trying to trick myself and the world," he said with tears in his eyes.

"Dear Pablito," replied Agustín, "Walking the path of the warrior is knowing that we have no chance of achieving victory, but in spite of that we are obliged to try again and again.

It is like being at the foot of a great mountain, without equipment, without food, without help, and knowing that what we want is to reach the peak. When you clean your links with Spirit, you find what you need by the path. Doors open for you, but you also discover that the peak is much higher than you ever imagined. And when you reach what you thought was the peak, you find an even higher peak exists.

On the path many fall by the wayside. Absolute confidence in your personal power and great capacity to see your environment are necessary. One day, gazing at the landscape, you discover that you have already reached the peak. But you also discover that it no longer matters.

Look at this hole in the ground, this burrow. In my entire life I have never learnt as much as I have sleeping here, inside. I have learned everything that I already knew, but that I could never explain in words. You can trick me, but there is no way to trick our Mother Earth. Sooner or later all that you are returns to her. The Earth always knows the truth.

Travelling is useless if wherever we go we take the same problems, the same questions, and we give the same answers. It changes the names of the streets or the cities we visit, but all of them will always be the same. I love few people as I love you, but all my love will not move the human condition you are facing one millimetre. Among my apprentices, you are the one who aspires the highest. This means that your fall will be resounding and painful. We all fall at some point and it is hard for us to get up. We have no chance of winning. The only thing we can do is enjoy our best attempt to the maximum, grow, evolve and change so that we can enter into the marvellous journey of knowledge and the mysteries we find on the way. You are not alone, my friend, but you won't travel accompanied.

"Speak to us about self-deceit," asked Manolo Pablos, a man who had travelled from León to listen to Agustín.

"You are no longer a normal, everyday man; if you were, the most normal thing in the world would be for you to deceive yourself so that you could feel you were worth something. But you are an aspirant to consciousness, and you can no longer lie to yourself.

Deceiving yourself is being, feeling or living something that isn't the truth, whether inside or outside yourself. It is seeing problems where they don't exist or seeing terrible realities that we can dump our dark side onto. Perhaps you see problems in the world where they don't exist. Maybe you are only inventing them in your mind.

On deceiving ourselves, we negate the best in ourselves and the best of what the world has given us. If you are a warrior, you can't deceive yourself, because something in you warns you: 'you'll regret it'. There are ways of deceiving yourself, positively negating the dark side of reality. Now you know. Before you weren't to blame, but now you are, if you are conscious that you are deceiving yourself.

We suffer because the world isn't as we would like it to be, we suffer because things end, we suffer because the people we love die or stop loving us.

You have tasted too much of the path of the warrior. You know too much to be a normal, everyday man, you know without knowing how you know, you know but you still don't know how to apply what you know in your everyday world, you know that you still haven't applied your own knowledge. You don't yet know enough to be a man of knowledge. You begin to be very conscious of each time you deceive yourself, and you can no longer accept this."

Miguelito, an older apprentice from the south of Spain, asked Agustín about mediocrity.

"The mediocre person wants to grow but can't because he hasn't got anyone to rest on. He looks for someone to rest on. Your social environment is mediocre. The men who surround you only aspire to the dreams of the conformist. You, on the other hand, want more, but you don't find support. People can't support you in something they don't believe in. Support yourself, trust in yourself, and don't ask for advice. Dare to fulfil your dreams. You have to stop being a second-rate man and move on to being first-rate. The mediocre man venerates the second-rate man and therefore searches for a second-rate woman."

43

"And what can you tell us about the second-rate woman?" asked Petra.

"A second-rate woman knows what she wants but doesn't dare to achieve it. She justifies herself with a thousand excuses and is used to seeing problems where there aren't any. The second-rate woman doesn't find solutions; she finds more problems.

Her aspirations are primary and she aims, for example, to have at her side a 'little man, the least bad will do, but anyone in the end who offers economic, social and reproductive security'. The second-rate woman limits her sexual desire to that of her partner. It could be that she has absolutely no sexual desire, however she says nothing and lets her partner enter her. It is common to find a second-rate woman who feels raped by her husband and he, on hearing her suffer, thinks that she is enjoying sex.

The second-rate woman accumulates problems, to finally vomit them at life, dirtying those who surround her. A second-rate woman looks for someone to resolve her life for her. She places no before yes, she has the vice of offering 'buts' in any situation she faces, lets opportunities pass her complaining that she isn't ready to take them. She complains, criticizes and condemns, and she loves criticizing herself, thinking that she is above or below the rest.

The second-rate woman compares herself to others, and in the comparison she loses her confidence in herself. She is used to seeing more defects than virtues, and she finds it hard to forgive defects. In this way she cultivates latent bitterness, which shows in her face. She is easily disappointed because of her expectations of others to foster her happiness."

Then Agustín handed Petra a list about the 'second-rate woman', and he asked her to underline in red all the sentences that described her, in green all those things she wanted to stop being, and in blue all those things that she would never want to be.

"It's important,' he told her, 'that you understand that this list isn't intended to criticize you, but to give you direction. It can give you an idea of what you want to be and what you

44

don't want to be in this life. Promise me that you won't criticize yourself or get angry with yourself on reading it."

"I promise, Agustín' Petra assured him.

THE SECOND-RATE WOMAN

She criticizes.
She needs a man.
She waits until someone recognizes what she does; she
represses herself.
She begs for love.
She doesn't know what she wants and waits for someone
to tell her.
She only has confidence in herself if everyone around
her tells her she's right.
She's cloying.
She sells herself cheap.
She's dependant on the people who surround her.
She always has economic dependencies.
She's at war with money.
She considers others to be to blame for her misfor-
tunes.
She waits for others to resolve her life, and if they
don't, she feels offended.
She's moralistic and repressed.
She's trapped in the problems of the past and desires
an impossible future.
She detests her present and is searching for a future
to avoid reality.
She lives by 'I suppose'.
She hates men because of her personal experiences of the
past.
She doesn't want to see how she is manipulated. She
waits for a miracle to occur in her favour.
She hates social machismo.
She chooses the least bad of the men that want her.
She gets depressed if she is alone.
She criticizes herself to saturation point.
She is resentful; she never forgives.
She wants to be a slave; she wants someone to direct her
life.
She is jealous.

Her jealousy leads her to enslave her loved ones.
She wants emotional exclusivity.
She believes everything she is told.
She argues without analysing.
She is mean.
She is traitorous.
She feels enslaved in the social group she belongs to.
She complains.
She feels undeserving.
She feels guilty.
She worries about humanity but does nothing.
She is envious. She doesn't like what she considers to
be more beautiful than her.
She is an accomplice to your weaknesses and doesn't support you in your growth.
She is destructive, even in her initiatives.
She doesn't feel ready, doesn't dare.
She is afraid of making mistakes.
She sabotages herself before reaching success.
She is clumsy and insecure.
She feels ashamed of herself.
For her, her pain is unbearable and the pain of others
is an exaggeration.
She looks for someone to take responsibility for her.
She feels ugly.
She doesn't look after herself.
She is nervous.
She carries around problems that aren't hers.
She is good or bad.
She knows how to find defects in people.
She limits herself in everything.
She thinks rubbish.
Her thoughts get out of control.
She is trapped in her first sexual relationship.
She emphasises her defects.
She hates others to mention her defects.
She lowers her head to those people she considers superior to her.
She neglects her family and demands stupid things.
She is compulsive.
She doesn't know how to be a mother.
She wants children so she has someone to control.
She has useless, dependant, immature children.

46

She has an adolescent as a partner.
She plays the role of putative mother.
She regrets her actions.
She avoids acting, with the justification of not harming anyone.
She is stupid.
She is aggressive when she wants to advance her objectives and afterwards has feelings of guilt and regret.
Every time she has an objective she misses it and then moans about it.
She speaks a lot but she says nothing.
She's like a corridor, men pass by but none of them stay.
She lives as best she can.
She survives.
She'd like to be someone else.
She compares herself to others to criticize herself and her world.
She denies her virtues.
When faced with an evident failure she prefers not to try to change her destiny.
She wants to be a first-rate woman but she thinks she isn't capable of it; that it is too big a challenge and so she doesn't try.
She is born as a second-rate woman and she resigns herself to being second-rate.
She has complexes and is heavy and complicated.
She knows how to ruin the most beautiful situations.
She knows how to miss opportunities and then she justifies herself.
She takes herself too seriously.
She thinks that men are either saviours or tyrants.
She is careless and out of control in her feelings.
She doesn't understand anything about men.
She frightens men.
She doesn't know how to fight for her objectives.
She is hard but fragile; the slightest thing breaks her.
She defends everything. She will attack or assault for the slightest reason.
She justifies herself.
She doesn't know how to take decisions.
She doesn't know how to say 'yes'.
She doesn't know how to say 'no'.

"And what is a first-rate woman?" asked Petra again.

"A first-rate woman has confidence in herself, even when everyone else doubts, even when she makes mistakes. She is a born fighter. She aspires to more than a little man, which means that she can reach the place where there are complete men and choose the best of them, who is hers by right.

The first-rate woman is open to new challenges, and is happy and sensual. She never has sexual relations unless she has real sexual desires, and she never does so out of obligation.

The first-rate woman enjoys life, she lives the life that she wants to live, is an accomplice to her partner without being an accomplice to his defects, she knows how to live her life and let others live theirs."

"Please Agustín, tell me more', asked Petra, "I need to understand this better."

"The first-rate woman is an exquisite being. She is a living unit, conscious of herself and in the process of internal and external growth. Aspiring to be a first-rate woman gives you direction in your feminine world without interference from the masculine world. It is a map. One thing connects you to another and you end up reaching the centre of your femininity with confidence in yourself above all."

Agustín got out another list and he asked her to under-line in red and blue respectively the concepts that she could identify with and those that she aspired to.

THE FIRST-RATE WOMAN

- She has a man and she enjoys him.
- She achieves her objectives.
- She doesn't need a man.
- She knows what she wants and how she wants it.
- She has confidence in herself in spite of her doubts.
- She is kind.
- She is a lady.
- She is independent.
- She knows how to resolve her economic situation.
- She is at peace with money.
- She accepts her responsibilities and acts according to

GREAT

48

her responsibilities.
- She is sensual and sexual.
- She can see her future and she knows how to live her present.
- She enjoys her present. The future and the past are only points of reference.
- She knows how to talk about a topic without getting distracted. She is specific.
- She recognizes when she is manipulated and she takes her own decisions.
- She understands animal machismo.
- She makes a good choice of men as her companions.
- She can be alone with herself.
- She has learnt to be her own friend.
- She knows how to forgive.
- She knows how to be free.
  She trusts her thoughts about her partner.
- She doesn't take slaves.
- She doesn't limit her love to one person.
- She is cultured.
- She knows how to analyse without arguing.
- She is sympathetic.
- She is upright.
- She is home-loving.
- She knows how to find the advantage in every situation.
- She wants to, she can and she deserves to.
- She is amiably indifferent.
- She offers something to humanity.
- She is happy.
- She is friendly.
- She loves beauty.
- She supports you in your best intention.
- She is creative.
- She has initiative.
- She overcomes fear of failure.
- She overcomes fear of success, and triumphs.
- She is sweet and gentle, but secure.
- She knows how to look you in the face.
- She has an intense life.
- She controls herself.
- She feels attractive.
- She cares for herself, looks after herself, and treats herself.
- She is peaceful.

- She resolves her problems.
- She is impeccable. She does things well. She knows how to walk 'the knife edge'.
- She knows how to find virtues in people.
- She knows how to overhaul her social, cultural, spiritual and moral limits.
- She has high quality thoughts.
- She has mental peace.
- She is orgasmic.
- She knows how to handle herself within eroticism.
- She knows how to polish her virtues.
- She knows how to hear about her defects without getting angry.
- She lowers her head to no one.
- She looks after her family without expecting thanks.
- She knows how to control her feelings.
- She is an exceptional mother.
- She has independent, mature and responsible children.
- She has a healthy, happy family.
- She has a man as a partner, not an adolescent adult.
- She plays the role of wife and companion.
- She never regrets.
- She lives her life without feeling very important.
- She doesn't have bad intentions.
- She uses her guile to achieve her objectives; she has no compassion.
- Once she has trapped her objective she keeps her hold.
- She knows what she is saying.
- She knows how to flirt with a man, how to catch him, hold him and be happy with him.
- She has a strategy to follow.
- She lives a life that is worthwhile.
- She is proud of being who she is.
- She knows how to use comparisons to enrich her life.
- She recognizes her limitations.
- She accepts her destiny with humility.
- She knows how to change her destiny, but she has no expectations.
- She knows that it is a great achievement to be a first-rate woman, and she recognizes her desire to achieve it.
- She is not born being a first-rate woman; she makes herself a first-rate woman.
- She is an artist in her everyday life, an artist in her

relationship with others and an artist in her enjoyment.
She knows how to turn every situation into something
pleasant.
She knows how to trap opportunities.
She doesn't take herself very seriously; she knows how
to laugh at herself.
She knows how to treat men as human beings.
She treats people very carefully, beginning with her
loved ones.
She knows that men are natural cowards and she uses this
knowledge.
She attracts men.
She is a fighter, placing great effort in her works.
She is hard but fragile. She recognizes this and that
makes her light.
She doesn't defend herself, she makes herself invisible.
She doesn't justify herself.
She knows how to take decisions.
She knows how to say 'yes'.
She knows how to say 'no'.

"And what about first and second-rate men?" The question was from Wolfgang, who expressed his desire to know the difference, emphasizing "even if it hurts."

"Let's see Wolfgang. Men and women are different, they think differently and they feel differently. Man understands reality from a different place. The woman is more resistant and the man is stronger muscularly. The woman has a great comprehension of the cosmos and the man a great understanding of individuality.

Compare each pair of sentences. They correspond to the first-rate and second-rate man respectively."

FIRST AND SECOND-RATE MEN

He knows how to listen to people.
He always wants to be right, even when he knows he's
wrong.

He knows how to laugh at himself; he doesn't take himself very seriously.

He takes himself too seriously, and he is easily offended.

He is fruitful.
He always lacks something: economic, affective or existential.

He's patient.
He gets desperate easily: with himself, with the world and with his loved ones.

He considers a woman to be a human being, a conscious being; a being that deserves respect and admiration even if he can't understand her. (Not even God understands her!)
He considers a woman to be a thing to desire, a problem, a tool and an investment; at best a substitute mother.

He recognizes that men are cowards by nature.
He denies his cowardice; he blames others for his fears.

He is daring. In spite of his fear, he tries even if he makes mistakes.
He has fear of failure, ridicule and success.

He recognizes his fragility.
He hides his fragility.

From his adolescence he knows what will be his function in the world, what he will work as.
He waits to mature to know what it is he wants in life.
He prepares himself whilst never feeling ready.

He is tolerant and kind.
He is intolerant and bad tempered.

He observes
He criticizes.

He perceives reality in an objective impartial way.
He analyses after having made prior judgments.

He trusts in his value and his social success.
He trusts in others, is disappointed by his lack of

capacity and by the achievements of others.

He faces ridicule.
He doesn't act for fear of ridicule.

He is socially virile.
He is socially impotent.

He is sexually attractive, with a 'je ne sais quois'
Women reject him; he bores them.

He is sexually resistant.
He has premature ejaculation.

He lives the life that he wants to live.
He feels lost; he lives as others advise him to live.

He trusts in himself even if everyone doubts.
He needs the approval of others to feel OK with himself.

He is happy.
He is neurotic.

He looks after his body.
His body is in bad condition.

He is elegant.
He is scruffy.

He finishes what he starts.
He is mediocre. He never finishes what he starts.

He aspires to the highest.
He has no aspirations.

He cultivates his personal power.
He cultivates social power.

He is light in conversation.
He is heavy in conversation.

He is gentle and hard.
He is sticky and absorbent.

He is generous and disinterested.
He is tight and mean.

He nourishes the soul of those who are near him.
His company wears and tires.

He cares for what he loves.
He destroys what he loves.

He knows how to protect his territory.
He has no territory.

He is a leader by nature, he is free and he likes free
people.
He is easily enslaved. He looks for a lord or a slave.

He knows how to work in a team; he occupies his place
within a group.
He systematically sabotages group work.

He works and earns what he deserves.
He acts as though he works and they act as though they
pay him.

He is very clear about the form of his relationship with
his partner.
He takes patterns and tries to imitate them.

He tries to understand his partner.
He gets angry with his partner because she isn't what
he wants her to be.

He motivates his partner and he helps her to strengthen
her virtues.
He tells his partner her defects at the first opportunity and he believes that he's helping her.

He has a definite personality.
He has no personality; he's changeable.

He is entertaining.
He's boring.

He's friendly and helpful.

He's tiresome and lazy.

He is gentlemanly in his treatment of everyone.
He is rough, he isn't familiar with basic good manners, and he only tries to be gentlemanly when it is in his interests.

He is eloquent in his way of speaking.
He is vulgar and rude in his speech and behaviour.

He is generous towards himself and others without over-doing it or feeling obliged.
He is tight-fisted.

He is a good friend.
He is suspicious.

He is interested in his fellow man.
He is interested in himself first, then in himself, and finally in himself.

He is generous.
He is selfish.

He is romantic.
He is grotesque and coarse.

He is intelligent.
He is stupid.

He is cultured.
He is ignorant.

He knows how to appreciate aesthetics and demonstrate his appreciation.
He appreciates nothing beyond his desires and obses-sions.

He is sensual.
He is pornographic.

He is sexual, an artist in bed, and he knows how to please his partner.
He is premature and he justifies his lack of sexual

capacity.

He knows how to play with words; he knows how to point out your mistakes without hurting you.
When he speaks of his feelings, he hurts others.

He is protective. People feel loved, cared for and understood by him.
You have to defend yourself from him. People approach him carefully.

He inspires confidence.
He inspires fear. You know you will regret being in his company.

He is creative.
He is apathetic.

He knows how to take time to rest.
He looks for time to be lazy and then he justifies himself.

He looks after himself; he is a friend to himself.
He commits excesses, he doesn't care for himself, and he is self-destructive and angry with himself.

He is noble.
He is traitorous.

He is a one-woman man.
He doesn't know how to maintain a stable relationship.

He is congruent.
He is incongruent.

He is loyal.
He is a liar.

He is a good businessman.
He loses in business.

Then Agustín asked Wolfgang and Petra to exchange their lists and to examine them – Petra from her masculine

56

side, and Wolfgang as if he were a woman.

"Speak to us about frustration," asked Esther, an English woman who lived in London

"Frustration eats away at you like acid, entering the deepest part of you. Some people dress themselves in armour on suffering its effects, but they become heavy, and they end up taking themselves very seriously. The shaman takes frustration with a large dose of laughter. He laughs at himself and accepts his karma. And if he needs to, he cries, even though he knows that his tears won't change his destiny.

Frustration is accompanied by bitterness; everything loses its taste, and everything you do has a shade of negativity.

Frustration needs small triumphs and short-term results. When you lose your hopefulness and live a borrowed life, rather than the one you should be living, frustration finishes you off little by little. By the time you realize, you no longer have the energy to change your life, and then you regret everything you have ever done, losing your memory of all your marvellous moments.

To end frustration you must begin by writing your album of sublime moments – a book that collects together your most beautiful experiences and stories so that they can rescue you in the very moment that frustration wants to trap you. Your album of sublime moments can be the exit door, but for it to work you must have written it, not only as beautiful memories, but also with beautiful words."

"Speak to us about sexuality," said Merche, shyly coming closer.

"The shaman uses as his foundation sexual energy, the telluric energy that links the heart of Mother Earth to the base of the spinal column. We raise this energy until it becomes Kundalini, which gives a feeling of vitality within the everyday world.

The specialized management of sexual energy is divided into two completely separate kingdoms:

1. The use, channelling and management of sexual

energy, with or without sexual activity.

2. The art of the 'pillow game', the meeting of partners: sensuality, sexuality and eroticism.

The shaman places sensuality before sexuality. He needs sexual energy to dream or travel through the Universe, to have good luck and to achieve what he wants.

Sexual wear and tear isn't produced during the sexual act itself, but rather before and after. It is generated by obsessions, courtship, compulsion, caprice, curiosity, morbidity or possessiveness. Pornography causes great harm to our sexual energy. The shaman runs from it like the plague."

"I'll explain a little to you of what the 'pillow game' is for shamans," continued Agustín. "The shaman understands that contact between the penis and the vagina creates an almost unbreakable connection.

The shaman always thinks 10 times before having a complete 'pillow game'.

The shaman knows that the emptiness that a woman feels is filled through the heart, not the vagina.

He knows that a woman can value a good hug more than a good lover.

The shaman first has a meeting with a woman in his dreams.

After that they make love with the soul.

Later they enter the 'pillow game': sensuality and the tips of the fingers.

Afterwards he romps with the woman as if he himself was a woman, without using his masculine organ.

In continuation he melts his masculinity, which is unity, with her femininity, which is the universe, but they don't explode in orgasm.

Finally the woman travels through madness and pleasure; she projects into to universe. And afterwards the man looks for his own explosion.

They return to sensuality.

After the 'pillow game', the nature of woman drives her to talk to her partner, whilst the tendency of the man is to relax, but he confuses this relaxation with falling asleep."

58

"Speak to us about love," requested Iris.

"The shaman understands that love is just one more energy in the Universe: the most exquisite, abstract, and the most desired by the human being, but also the rarest.

Everything the shaman does he glues together with love, appealing always to impeccability.

For a western person, loving is synonymous with worrying. The shaman doesn't worry; he takes care of his loved ones.

The shaman cannot limit his love to one single person. Neither does he think that love is forever. He struggles to avoid associating love with suffering, or need. He never believes stories of the type 'the more I love you, the more I suffer'.

Even though the object of his love disappears, the love itself is an energy that lasts. When the shaman loves, he has no need for the object or the person he loves to manifest love to him.

Love for the shaman isn't a business deal, it isn't 'I'll only love you if you love me' nor 'I'll treat you well if you treat me well'. He doesn't buy love with gifts, compliments or demonstrations of love. The shaman is not a buyer of affection.

Showing love is always a gesture to Spirit, and the shaman does not ask for recognition or gratitude in return.

The love of the shaman is one of the most exquisite and difficult tasks in the world. The shaman doesn't believe in love, he tries to experience it, demonstrate it and witness it. He mistrusts words full of love or people who justify or shield themselves in love."

"Please speak to us about love for the partner," asked Lidia, the woman who Agustín loved.

"Just as we talked about love in general, love between partners also exists in two different ways.

1. There is the commercial love, of exchange and buying and selling: 'I'll love you as long as you love me' or 'I love you and, as you don't appreciate me, I use my love to cause you pain'.

2. The love of the shaman is unconditional love, love for

the sake of love. A love without beginning or end: 'I love you even if you don't love me' and 'if you don't love me I won't suffer and I'll continue loving you'. This is the love that I want to believe in.

Loving you for me is entering into the knowledge of your most intimate secrets and supporting you in your best intention. Love isn't words. It is a feeling that transmits strength and security. It is a feeling that razes everything but ends up strengthening.

Commercial love is only fruitful when there is exchange. If one of the two stops loving, it is consumed by itself: suffering arrives, anger, desperation and loss. Commercial love is limited to people who pertain to our same social class.

Unconditional love is manifested with ease without mattering who or how we love. It goes way beyond social categories. You can fall in love with and have a partner belonging to another class, however far from yours.

Unconditional love frees you from all barriers, but it is not something that manifests itself freely. Unconditional love doesn't oblige you to love anybody. It is an exquisite pleasure and it is never exclusive.

When a shaman has a partner, his pleasure and obligation is to love her exactly as she wants to be loved, support her in her best intention, use all his capacity to help her find her path and fulfil her destiny, even though this leads to loss or separation from the loved one⋯"

"You and I," concluded Agustín, addressing himself to his loved one, "may possibly never be a couple, but I know that I can't die without showing you how much I love you."

"Speak to us about sadness," asked Manuela.

"Sadness, to the eyes of the seer, is a beautiful blue light in the chest, a large bubble that holds the emptiness most highly prized by the shaman. Sometimes this bubble has to crack and this creates a feeling like something breaking in the chest. It is a pain of the soul that feels like it will kill us, and is accompanied by great sighs.

Sadness is a feeling that brings with it nostalgia and longing. It is the consciousness of our body knowing that one day

60

we won't be in this marvellous world any longer, and that from that day on we won't be able to show our love for the people we love. Sadness leads us to appreciate what we are and what we will stop being.

Sadness invites us to be creative. It moves us to write a poem, paint a painting, compose music, give a hug, express our love to a loved one.

When this totally creative, pure feeling of the soul generates a crack so strong that you feel like you are dying, you must lie down on the ground and let the Earth absorb your pain. But, above all, when this happens to you with such force, let it carry you and see where it takes you. Then form it into something concrete. Whatever.

The western world has limited the feelings of the soul by educating us to be fearful of sadness and emptiness. We were tricked when we were made to believe that sadness is a synonym of depression."

"Speak to us about depression," said Rosa, who had suffered depression on many occasions.

"Depression is a mental process: we need words in our mind to fall into it. Depression is the fruit of out-of-control, negative and critical thoughts. It is produced when the dark side of reality filters into the thoughts of a person and ends up trapping them.

One day you are happy, and then you suddenly discover critical thoughts about yourself or your world. These thoughts lay the foundations for a sensation of anxiety, heaviness, failure or uncertainty.

Your own thoughts seem strange to you but, if you permit them to repeat themselves again and again, you end up identifying them as yours. The worst thing is that you believe them··· That is when the dark side of reality has cornered you.
"

"But what can be done against it?" asked Rosa, with a look of pain on her face.

"Discipline is the only thing that distances the dark side from your thoughts. Mental discipline. You have to recognize that those thoughts aren't yours and not pay them any attention. Try to get depressed without thinking⋯. It's impossible.

Have the discipline to choose your own thoughts or, even better, don't think anything. 'This criticism is not mine⋯ out of me. This painful thought doesn't belong to me. I don't have to believe what I think. This depression travels with me, but it isn't part of me, out of me.' Ignoring depression helps your energy to re-establish itself.

The dark side of reality feeds off the energy that you waste on this out of control train of depressive thoughts. You must simply stop feeding it: ignore the thoughts; turn around when you hear them. Let yourself be carried away by an action, but above all avoid sitting down and thinking.

Use any of the directive sentences to enter into a positive state of thought; it doesn't matter if you consider the sentence to be a lie at that moment. Repeat positive things in the present/future: 'From now on I'm going to feel better, better and better. Every day it is easier for me to control my thoughts positively. With each moment my happiness in life increases.'

Repeat these sentences some hundred times a day, even if you don't believe in them. The important thing is to repeat them with power."

"Why do sadness and nostalgia go hand in hand?" asked Carmen and Angi, two sisters from Germany.

"Nostalgia is the effect of our cosmic and genetic memories of the most marvellous moments of our existence as consciousness. We feel nostalgia for our old home, as much from this life as from others. We even long for our distant home in the stars.

Allowing yourself be carried away by nostalgia is remembering your most powerful moments, and this offers you the possibility of bringing them into the present and soaking you in their power. But reason won't accept these memories as truthful, so your subconscious disguises them as fantasy and imagination.

Longing is a feeling that arises from the ancestral wisdom that you have, but that you don't know how to use."

"Agustín, speak to us about defects, vices and virtues," asked his beautiful, beloved sister, Ivonne.

"We all have vices and defects, but also virtues, and that is where it is in our interests to place our attention, to reinforce the strong side of each of us.

I suggest forgiving at least three defects in the people you love and, in addition, praising three virtues. In this way you will be loved and welcomed everywhere.

It is also convenient to remember that what we consider to be defects may be considered virtues by others, and vice versa.

Speaking for myself, one of the things I consider to be a virtue is my fascination for female beauty. I love women and I am happy when I let them know the pleasure they give me and the love I have for them. For some, this is a defect simply because they don't consider it to be normal, and they don't approve of loving more than one woman at a time."

"Speak to us of the Great Spirit," requested Francesca, an English woman who often travelled to Spain to work with the shaman.

"I use the word Spirit because it is more abstract than God, Cosmos or Universal Energy. You could also say 'Giver of Life', or 'Taker of Consciousness'. The Great Spirit is more like the God of the fairies than the God of the Christians. The God of the fairies is called 'To Sungar', which means: 'That which asks nothing, but gives nothing, That which receives anything you want to give, and That which puts everything you need in the world for you to take'.

Spirit is unpronounceable, and can't be understood. It is manifested in everything in creation. It is That which exists, existed and will exist. We can't, therefore, aspire to understand it.

The shaman doesn't try to understand Spirit. He tries to witness it and understand its manifestations. He knows that understanding even the smallest part of the manifestations of Spirit requires great energy and absolute interior silence.

The shaman can enter the Akashic archives, where all the answers are kept, and understand the personal manifestations of Spirit towards his world or his personal vision of reality.

Spirit is too big to be understood."

"Speak to us of the world," asked Anton, Francesca's teenage son.

"Spirit, on creating all living beings, made them similar to him: of pure energy. The differences between races, sexes, and the different forms that consciousness takes are only interpretations. We are exclusively energy. All the animals of the woods, the plants and the spirits are our brothers, because they are the children of the Great Spirit.

The blood of the rivers is our blood. The Earth is our body, our womb. We are children of the Earth, and we belong to her, she doesn't belong to us.

Nothing belongs to us. Our body, our material things, our loves and our family are all lent to us. Everything is offered to us so that we can look after it, and everything must be returned one day. It is our obligation to return it in a good state.

The world where we exist has consciousness and this consciousness becomes conscious of us when we become conscious of the world, conscious that we are alive, and that we are going to die."

"Speak to us of the path of the shaman," asked Christopher Robinson, an English pupil who lived in Andalusia.

"The path of the shaman is not a religion. Nor is the shaman a guru or religious leader. The shaman is only the porter who opens the door so that you, with your energy, can continue your path, your personal road. The shaman is not interested in anyone following his life, because he believes that everyone should live his or her own life. But he is interested in finding good plots to plant in, or people with good energy with whom he can walk a stretch of his path.

The shaman is an intermediary between the energy of Spirit and that of the human being. The shaman is a human being who doesn't search for glorification, but rather that people see that it is possible to reach a place of balance between the everyday world and the magical world. He is only there, on stage, so that the world knows that it is possible.

The path of the shaman isn't something to believe in, it is something to live; it isn't dogma, or faith, nor is it a doctrine: it is a path. And to walk it the shaman needs energy and confidence – in himself, and in the mandates of the Sprit towards him – as well as dedication to the process of cleaning of his connection to Spirit.

The shaman doesn't doubt, yet he questions everything, even himself, especially when he knows that a private vice exists near him. Little by little this questioning is changed into an absolute certainty about what is and what is not. Even then he continues to question.

He knows that his life is a paradox; that a single path crosses in different places at the same time. The contradiction confronts him at every turn and he has to convert it into the art of the paradox.

The shaman does not judge, nor criticize nor condemn. He knows that he is in no position to determine what is going on with other people."

"Agustín," asked Sophia with her English accent, "what can you tell us about couples?"

"The woman is like a triangle with the point facing downwards. She sets off from one point and is projected into the infinite. The man is like a triangle with the point facing upwards, he sets off from any place and he has an objective, but he is limited in the point of the pyramid. The man gives direction and the woman gives range.

What is difficult with a woman is not to project her into the infinite; it is to bring her back. Woman is abstract by nature. What is difficult with a man is projecting him, breaking the shell that limits him to a specific objective.

Women have double the energy of men by the fact of having a womb. Little by little the everyday man robs the woman of her confidence and self-esteem so that he can manipulate her. The man manipulates through words and emotional blackmail. The liberation of the woman begins when she realizes that it is impossible for the man to always be right.

The first objective of the shaman towards his partner is

to help her to re-establish her self-esteem, and to relocate her power in the centre, in her womb.

The shaman helps the woman to liberate the energy of her womb. The womb of the woman is like a second brain and is the nearest thing to God that man knows. But masculine manipulation has meant that this second brain is limited to reproduction and sexual pleasure.

· The intellectual thinks with his head.
· The Indian thinks with his heart.
· The male shaman thinks with his belly.
· The woman thinks with the womb.

When the woman thinks with the head she is confused, when she learns to think with the womb, understanding this without any sexual connotation, she reaches absolute certainty.

To reach absolute certainty and the knowledge of her power within the womb, the woman must free herself of the energy that men have left inside her vagina, and the energy that the social order has left in her through her children."

"Speak to us of the woman," asked Paquy.

"A woman is like the rose that perfumes the foot of the person who steps on it.

The shaman collects the trodden flowers that he finds on his path and he puts them in the vase of his life with the water that flows from his heart. When the flower puts out roots, the shaman returns it to the Earth.

A woman is to be contemplated, just like a flower. She is to be loved without desire and wanted without profanation. A woman should be treated as a human being, not a woman.

The shaman is a gentleman, but he doesn't treat a woman like an idiot.

Whenever he can he offers a compliment, to delight the thoughts of the woman."

"Speak to us of invocations and spells," asked Daisy, a young pupil.

"The word of the shaman has power. He avoids speaking, and if he speaks, he does it with flourish, or with the voice of

Spirit. He is very careful with what he says because he knows that anything can be turned into reality. If you invoke rubbish, then you are granted rubbish; if you invoke something that is worthwhile, then worthwhile things are granted to you.

Each of us should be very careful and ask ourselves whether what we say is what we want to say, or if we will regret it. In order to learn to invoke words with power, we must have quality thoughts. We manifest our thoughts, but as we don't know that the world can be conscious of what there is in our mind, we let it run away with us.

Imagine, Daisy, that Agustín could read your thoughts: would you feel ashamed of yourself, or would you be proud of what you think? This questioning will open the door of quality thoughts to you, and therefore quality invocations."

"Speak to us of change," requested Merry, Daisy's older sister.

"There are two basic situations that can produce change. When someone feels bad, tired or out of place, changing allows them to survive, whereas if the starting point is consciousness of the self, change leads to real evolution. This is the change that the apprentice pursues.

Change and sadness are the joining of our evolution and longing for the being that we have to become, with the nostalgia for the best of ourselves of an earlier life.

Change has to be gentle, gradual, harmonious and very discreet. Throughout the process you need to take into account that it is probable that the people who love you won't like the fact that you are changing your way of being, feeling, thinking or dressing.

Your loved ones don't want you to become an unknown, even if you are healthier. They will prefer you to be as you were, even if you were mediocre.

'I prefer you mediocre and familiar, to healthy and unknown' they may think.

An unknown is difficult to manipulate or emotionally blackmail. Learn to behave in a 'normal' way towards the people who love you.

Change is an art that needs large doses of elegance and

discretion. When the work of art is ready, you exhibit it to the world so that they can marvel at what you have done to yourself. It isn't easy. Like everything, it has its price. We live in a predatory Universe, where nothing is for free. What you consider a gift is in reality an achievement of your personal power and the impeccability of your life."

"And what do I give to Spirit?"- asked Merry.

"A payment for the wonderful world you were born in. When you are finally facing your death and you say goodbye, you will know if you paid for everything beautiful that life gave you and you will know if you took everything exquisite that life offered you. Now you have to change everything to prepare yourself for that moment. It's your choice."

"What is the dark side of reality?" asked their Japanese friend, Maho worriedly.

"The dark side of reality feeds off our energy. It traps our consciousness and it places it at the most enslaved, low and limited levels possible. Self-importance leads us to venerate the dark side of reality in the most subtle or blatant way and to totally deny the light side of our perception.

This dark side has its bearers, which we call predators of consciousness. They are energetic masses that are conscious of themselves, that use our perceptual limitations to manipulate our energy, filtering into our thoughts in the most ingenious ways.

In the confusion of our social order, they succeed in stopping us from distinguishing between our thoughts and theirs. Not everything we think belongs to our consciousness or our true selves, nor is every thought we think ours. We have to learn to distinguish between our thoughts and those that aren't ours; which thoughts belong to us and where the rest come from.

The dark side shouts, speaks and gatecrashes our thoughts, distancing our own voice of consciousness. Not everything we think comes from us. The dark side uses its emissaries to infiltrate. The predators use our own mental voice and in this way they manage to control our consciousness. The predators, once introduced in our thoughts, feelings and emotions, dictate the majority of what we consider to be our desires and needs.

Two types of thought exist: those of the predators and those that belong to our true self. The second of these is what we call absolute certainty.

The thoughts of the dark side and the predators speak constantly in our mind, filling us with confusion. Absolute certainty is a small voice that we have limited by putting it into a corner of our consciousness. Absolute certainty speaks once and then is silent.

The shaman spends his life cleaning his connection to this certainty so that he can distinguish it within the tangle of thoughts that nest in the human mind.

The predators use the primary states to coerce us mentally, making a consensus in our desires, which facilitates the process of slavery. The primary states are reproduction, feeding, relationships and the ecosystem in which we live; they dictate the social consensus. The dark side has created social consensus, aligning human consciousness in agreement with social entities.

The light side of reality wants to open perceptual doorways and allow us to recover the consciousness of our cosmic origins."

"Speak to us of self-importance," asked Lulu, an English pupil.

"Self-importance searches for a way to enslave you to a concept, a person, a moral, or a view of reality. In this way it denies you the possibility of discovering that there are an infinite number of ways of perceiving freedom.

I'll summarize it in the way that I have understood it. Self-importance is:

Always speaking about yourself.

Defending and sustaining your dark side.

Feeling responsible for the misfortunes and problems of others.

Needing recognition.

Needing the world to know you exist.

Believing yourself to be special and that you have a special task in the world.

Feeling yourself to be an entity separate from your social or natural environment.

Self-importance obliges you to catalogue everything as good or bad.

Self-importance leads you to invest your energy in your fellows so that at the first opportunity you can get back what you've invested, with interest.

Self-importance is like a business card that tells the world how you want to be labelled, where you want to catalogue yourself.

Self-importance enslaves you to your image of yourself and closes the doors to transformation and evolution.

Self-importance isn't bad; it is simply a characteristic of wear and tear or a waste of energy."

Pau was a Catalan apprentice who showed signs that he would no longer continue approaching him to learn. Agustín understood that the soul of Pau knew that he wouldn't return, although his consciousness still hadn't recognized it. This filled him with sadness. Pau didn't realize that the chat that he was going to have with Agustín was a goodbye. Agustín looked at him and he knew that his time with him had ended. He asked him to help clean one of the nests that they had built between them in the middle of the forest. The nest consisted of canvas stretched over three poles tied between three tree tops, suspended seven metres high, made comfortable with straw and blankets, and resting on a network of climbing ropes. It was a true nest for humans.

"Speak to me about your sadness, Agustín" asked Pau.

"Sadness gives shine to my eyes. When it was born I cultivated it and protected it from depression. I knew that depression would try to annihilate my sadness and I learned to differentiate between the two of them easily."

Agustín wanted to emphasize the difference between them and the need to avoid confusing them.

"Depression destroys, criticizes and makes you fight against yourself. Pau fights Pau and Pau loses. Depression is accompanied by emotion, and you can't have emotions without thinking. To get depressed you need to think, criticize, attack yourself, complain, and think that no one understands you. You can't enter the dark side of reality without thinking, until you are overwhelmed. Depression was made by the dark aside to destroy.

Sadness, on the other hand, is a feeling of the soul, it invites you to be creative, it beautifies you, and it cleans you. Today my soul feels sad, I feel like crying, but I have no reason. This creativity invites me to act, to shape the best of myself, like in a beautiful conversation with you. Sadness is like the memory that one day I will die, it reminds me that perhaps this nest is the last thing that I will do in this life. This sadness and that consciousness make me enjoy the moment and give the best of myself in this instant.

One day you will go, Pau, and you should let sadness give you direction, teach you how to give thanks in your heart, so that your words and your acts know how to show gratitude for how beautiful life has been for you. Sadness will help your destiny rescue you from mediocrity, and everything that you have experienced with me will be nothing compared to the beautiful voyage that awaits you.

If you let yourself go with depression you will live regretting what you lost in the shamanic world; you will lose your gains, your treasure of knowledge and the best of your memories of these two years of struggle."

Pau cried in the nest that he loved so much. Agustín knew that in this instant his destiny was written.

And so, people from all over continued to come to speak to Agustín, to ask him to read their aura, to discover the marvellous side of life, to use joy as a path of knowledge··· and Agustín received them and gave them advice, at the same time as he allowed them to live unforgettable moments among those beautiful mountains of the Catalan pre-Pyrenees, with Nature as teacher and trees as brothers.

The people helped him to haul stones, they met in the tipi, and they danced to the rhythm of the drums···

In this way, Agustín became the gardener who cares for

his flowers, in a garden where shamans flowered, where eyes shone, and faces glowed with joy.

Creating a garden of healthy, beautiful beings had become the task of the shaman.

THE PATH
OF KNOWLEDGE

gustín had six apprentices who were more advanced: Luís Manolito, Luís 'Toc Toc', Joanna, Christopher Robinson, Verena and Petra. They had worked hard enough for Agustín to give them a small manual on shamanism. They were happy, above all Luis, who floated in the clouds. The other prospective apprentices laughed affectionately at his pride and joy at knowing that they were working well.

It was very interesting for everyone to see the expression on the faces of the others as they read the manual for the shaman's apprentice. On seeing them Agustín relived his own history as an apprentice to José. Speaking with his apprentices was a balm to his soul; it made him remember the beautiful way that José had led him for so many years, without him becoming aware of his manipulation.

He really missed José every time anyone asked him anything and he remembered those computer printouts, those winter afternoons in the Mexican mountains.

MEMORIES OF JOSÉ,
AGUSTÍN'S BENEFACTOR

We were in San Pablo Axu, the Sierra del Aguila in the

Mixteca Mountains, in Oaxaca. José and myself were accompanied by a cousin of mine called Iván and his father, the municipal president of Uaxuapan, Don Rafael Orea.

José got out a manuscript from a wooden trunk. While he was searching and moving things around, I could see, amongst the papers, old codices that the Mixtecos kept hidden from anthropologists. Some were covered with leather and others looked like recent copies.

He handed me some photocopies of a computer printout.

"Modern, we shamans are," he said as he winked at me.

I sat down on a crate of milk that I usually used as a seat.

A smiling girl of about seven, who I later found out was José's niece, arrived at the house. He asked me for a floppy disk. Sometimes I carried a laptop with me, and José liked to use a floppy to 'clean', carrying out a shamanic healing on children by passing it close to their body. Afterwards he turned on the computer and while he showed them a programme with psychedelic colours, he assured them that they were cured. That's what he did with this girl, who had a stomach-ache and a low fever.

Meanwhile I read the papers that he had given me. I was used to his game, I knew that he would ask me to turn on the computer with the colourful programme and he would tell the girl that she was now cured.

I was interested in the document:

'SHAMANIC CODE OF PRACTICE
WITHIN THE BLUE LINEAGE'.

"I wrote it for you," José told me, whilst I read:

Applied Shamanism
Practical knowledge
of the shamans of the third millennium
The beginning of the sixth sun

Shamanism is not the exclusive property of anyone. It is neither a religion nor a dogma. It is a solitary path that each participant walks.
The shaman is an empty tube through which Spirit descends, he is a servant of Spirit and he simply humbly

74

obeys the designs of power.

The shaman is a normal person who, through discipline
and impeccability, has made his world into a beautiful
and magical world.

The shaman has a code and he reinvents this code according to his circumstances and his pacts with Spirit.

José was enjoying watching me read the manuscript.

"Let's see what you make of this," he said, pointing to the
second part of the document.

"Is this serious José?" I asked incredulously, as I read.

"Of course. Read it carefully. Although you don't believe
it, this is your destiny," he assured me.

I really couldn't believe what José wanted me to do in
Europe, and I carried on reading···

"…Cosmovision and understanding of the way of tackling
hierarchies and functions within the Blue group, to form
and create a seed of knowledge in Europe…"

indicated the text.

According to José's papers, the 4 conditions needed by
the apprentice for entering the path of knowledge were:

Respect

Discretion

Impeccability

Discipline

And a series of categories was necessary within the centre for
shamanic development:

Participant: one or two years of continuous apprenticeship.

Coordinator: prepares courses and talks, and helps to
organize the events.

Helper: participates as a helper on the courses.

Kojai (shaman's helper): has responsibilities within the
group.

Sensei: is capable of working with a group and giving
classes.

Apprentice: someone given over to shamanic knowledge,

under the protection of a benefactor.
Shaman: capable of regrouping his consciousness and that of his apprentices.

Each aspirant who wants to enter the shamanic world has to pay the price of knowledge. He knows that knowledge works as an energetic business and tries to understand the rules, to be able to master them.
For each aspirant the price is different, just as each personal universe is.
Each of the categories is managed with different rules and the aspirant to knowledge has the pleasure of trying to discover why Spirit manifests in this business with him.
Money, favours, love, knowledge will never be enough to pay for everything that the shaman's apprentice takes from Spirit, but at the same time it isn't necessary to pay in this way. There is a place in the apprenticeship where the apprentice pays with consciousness.
A complete apprentice knows that the best way to manifest his thanks is by raising his consciousness and manifesting it in his everyday world.
He is conscious of how he is tempted by the dark side of reality; how he is trapped by the predators of consciousness.
He is conscious of his search and of his hunger for knowledge.
He is conscious of which thoughts belong to him, and which don't.
He is conscious that he has more opportunities than problems.
Consciousness permits him to fall in love with life.
Consciousness permits him to live a life that is worthwhile, the life that he has always wanted to live, a life with heart.
His consciousness permits him to express his understanding and stop it, if that is his wish.
At the beginning of his apprenticeship, consciousness takes the apprentice to a place called the impotence of wisdom: he knows but he still doesn't know how to apply what he knows.
Consciousness has its price. When we don't know, we are free, but once we know we can't lie to ourselves.

76

CATEGORIES

PARTICIPANT: a person who attends seminars, participates in a conference, or receives a therapy and could be interested in the shamanic path. They have been trying the path for more than a year.

COORDINATOR: the intermediary within the social order, between Spirit and participants, bringing new apprentices nearer and creating the necessary means of diffusion and economy.

HELPER (Cocoa seed): a person who wants to give and learn through giving. He is more interested in helping than in being helped. He helps disinterestedly and understands that his apprenticeship is to watch the process of the participants in order to identify himself, remember his own process and have a different vision of the circumstances.

The helper knows that he is there to serve rather than to be served. He no longer looks for the care of the instructor, but instead supports the other apprentices in their best choice. He doesn't go around looking for help, but rather helps and in this way he discovers new ways to learn. He has the opportunity to see the apprenticeship from another point of view.

KOJAI (Ocelot helper): the helper of the shaman teacher…

José invited me to continue reading carefully so that I could try to catalogue myself in one of the categories. I tried to concentrate but something inside or outside wanted to distract me into thinking rubbish. I carried on reading the characteristics that defined what the manual called the 'Kojai'.

The Kojai has the pleasure of accepting the obligation of being strong, of not abandoning himself to weakness. The Kojai has the capacity to be subjected to any type of test or situation of ridicule, because he knows how to control his feelings and his daring. It is possible to speak of his defects in public and it won't affect him because he no longer cares what others think of him. His strength, fruit of his saving of energy, permits him to:

> Control his desperation and convert it in energy.
> Convert tiredness into understanding.

Fear into unconcern.
Worry into active indifference.
Anger into a reserve of energy.
Fury into direction and personal power.

The Kojai is a helper who has achieved a minimum of control over his thoughts.

He knows how to distinguish which thoughts belong to him and which don't, which deserve attention, which are worth thinking and from where each thought comes.

He distinguishes between genetic thoughts and those of the predators.

The Kojai, little by little, becomes immune to wearing emotions, such as depression, jealousy, criticism, envy, hatred, impotence or frustration, amongst others.

He knows how to cultivate and take advantage of the feelings of the soul: emptiness, sadness, freedom, nostalgia, acceptance, longing, hunger for knowledge.

His mental strategies distance him from feeling pity for others and he only sees the best in every person.

He is never an accomplice to the weakness of others.

The Kojai doesn't defend himself; he has nothing to defend.

He has declared a truce with his ego, whose dangers he knows, and he keeps it at a distance.

The Kojai knows how to laugh at destiny, he knows how to laugh at his own problems, and he knows how to walk the beautiful edge of life.

The Kojai has created his own personal cosmovision of reality, he understands it and he respects it.

He has reworked his personal pacts with Spirit:

    Of love
    Of ethics
    Of relationships
    Of prosperity
    Of sexuality
    Of happiness
    Of money
    Of spirituality

He makes his personal pacts with Spirit and he knows how to take responsibility for those pacts.

The Kojai has great mental discipline, high quality thoughts and exquisite self-respect.

He has learned not to criticize himself. He observes and

cultivates personal impeccability.

The Kojai develops his capacity to learn in dreams, he awakes knowing, without knowing how he knows, remembering what he has been taught whilst sleeping.

The Kojai has to have a great capacity for improvisation and adaptation. He knows that every circumstance is different and every solution is an art.

The Kojai knows how to polish his virtues and use his defects.

The Kojai has to be:

Charming.

Helpful.

Friendly.

Attentive.

Happy.

Cultured.

Hard-working.

Grateful.

Decent.

Impeccable.

SENSEI (Eagle teacher): He doesn't teach because he thinks he knows more than the participants. He teaches because he understands that he has to teach what he is learning and commit himself to his own knowledge.

His words and acts are absolutely coherent.

He is a mystery, even to himself.

He sees... he knows without knowing how he knows.

He can distinguish the voice of seeing.

He can distinguish between when he is observing and when he is criticizing.

He knows how to speak with his feelings.

He tries to cross the borders of good and bad.

The law of impeccability rules him.

He has dismantled his social world and restructured it according to his personal vision.

To the eyes of the spectator he is a normal, harmonious person, a good and useful citizen.

He knows how to be at peace in both a wild and urban environment.

He has the capacity to teach in dreams.

It isn't important to him to understand what Spirit wants of him, he simply obeys, knowing that at some point absolute certainty will arrive.

APPRENTICE (the walker of Mayab): He is taken under the protection of a shaman, a benefactor or other responsible person. The apprentice has to untangle Spirit's strategy for his apprenticeship.
Sometimes these strategies are completely different and contrary. This helps the apprentice learn even when there is no apprenticeship.
When a participant, organizer or helper becomes an apprentice, he has to be very clear that he isn't a special person, that there are no spiritual privileges or privileges of consciousness; that he is neither better nor worse than any other aspirant to shamanism.

The text covered various pages that I examined, conscious that reading them would allow me to rework the direction of my apprenticeship. The characteristics of Kojai and Sensei deeply affected me, and I wanted to embody all the qualities attributed to them both. It was like a map of steps to take, of objectives to achieve.

As I read more I realized that the document had absolutely no indigenous connotations. It didn't even employ the terms that José used with me. I looked at it without understanding what was going on.

"I've written it according to your IQ, because if you can't understand it you won't be able to apply it," he said as he winked at me. I didn't know if he was teasing me.

I didn't like the idea of establishing categories at all. One of the things that had most convinced me about this shamanic lineage was what I considered to be the complete absence of categories or dogmas, but it seemed that I was wrong.

I looked at José and noticed that my lack of confidence in him increased as I watched him convincing the child of the curative effects of the computer programme, even though the healing was effective. I felt defrauded because, although I knew that his role as shaman was to create tricks so that people would cure themselves, I didn't like him manipulating me or using me⋯

"What's important is that she is cured and that she goes away happy," answered José, responding to my reflections.

I felt embarrassed when I realized that he was perceiving

my thoughts.

"You earn each category," he said, "this fits you like a shoe. No one can tell you whether you are a pupil or a teacher. Your anger at me is owing to the fact that you don't know where to place yourself within this list. You know that you are a little of all but you aren't completely any. Perhaps we should invent a category exclusively for you, and then you would be happy."

His certainty about things irritated me. He always seemed to have an answer for everything. I continued reading the Manual for a Third-rate Shaman.

MANUAL FOR A THIRD-RATE SHAMAN

Those that write manuals are second-rate, and first-rate shamans don't get involved in this kind of nonsense because they don't need manuals.

I knew that he was enjoying the expression on my face as I read what he had prepared for me. I liked his sense of humour and the way he laughed at his own knowledge.

"Learn this well," he told me, holding back his laughter.

All of this seemed more like leg pulling than serious work. I thought about my ten years of fruitless yet marvellous apprenticeship with José and I tried to force myself to understand what he was trying to teach me.

Principles:

1. A shaman never lies to himself.
2. A shaman never lies, but neither does he tell the truth.
3. He never takes the world, Spirit or himself seriously.
4. The shaman only obeys the mandates of Spirit; he knows how to be obedient.
5. The shaman knows that the shamanic path is something serious, but that he doesn't have to be serious.
6. The shaman, before carrying out his will, carries out

the will of Spirit, but he never uses intermediaries nor
other shamans. He either communicates directly with the
source or he knows how to listen to omens.
7. The shaman never steals, nor takes anything that
doesn't belong to him. He tries to live within rectitude, his own rectitude.
8. He never desires the woman of a friend.

   I was beginning to like what I was reading and I continued.

The process of apprenticeship

The shaman has a meeting with death. Death, physically
or symbolically, takes his soul, breaks it into pieces
and, if it feels that his life is in some way worthwhile, puts it back together again, placing everything
in a new order. Afterwards it replaces his soul in his
body.
On surviving the first battle with Death, everything is
identical yet nothing is the same.
Then he can be considered a shaman's apprentice.
Afterwards he has to confront his thoughts, silence them
and know how to recognize which are his and which are
not, and which are those of Spirit. And stop their overwhelming flow and the compulsion of digression and lack
of control.
Later feelings flower, and just like thoughts they over-
flow. He will battle with his feelings. On not thinking,
he won't know how to recognize the diversity of emotions
that are trapped in his body. Sadness will envelop him
until it almost kills him and the apprentice will only
have recourse to the Earth, or to letting himself go
with the flow of this sadness.
Between meeting and meeting, the apprentice will run
into magic, phenomenology and the mystery. He must cultivate any manifestation of Spirit but never, under any
circumstances, give it importance or use it as a subject for conversation or part of his presentation of
himself to the world. 'For his eyes only'.

Relationship with others

The shaman comes into this world not only to give, but

also to receive.

But he doesn't walk around trying to be good either.

The shaman isn't a good man, but neither is he a bad man. He is only the best of himself, as impeccable as he can be.

The shaman always plays at being beyond good and bad. He makes his decisions with fluidity within this game, and he makes them from the best of himself.

He doesn't try to be humble, but at the same time being important doesn't matter to him, he is simply the best of himself.

The shaman doesn't worry about his loved ones, nor does he fantasize about how to help them; rather he takes care of them through real acts, with the best of himself.

He supports others in their best purpose, from the best of himself.

The shaman doesn't try to impose his desire for freedom on others. He discovers what is the desire for freedom of those people who are with him and supports them in their personal intent, with all the best of himself.

The shaman is not an accomplice to the vices of others. He is the best of himself.

He is delicate and discriminating with the world, but he is ruled by his own, very personal code of conduct, which he has reworked based on this document: a system of rules that he himself has written listening to his own personal wisdom: a code to which he has given the best of himself.

The rest of the document consisted of about 50 blank pages entitled:

'Elaborate your own manual of shamanism, in writing'.

I looked at José – in this moment something in me changed. It was as if a heavy fog evaporated from my soul. I knew how to recognize these instants, when something in me got rid of a predator of consciousness. I had a clear understanding of why José played with me in this way. I laughed as hard as I could because I loved his irony and the joyful way he had of teaching me and pushing me to work.

I made a promise to myself to write my own manual for a second-rate shaman. I thought about the title. José looked at me with love and pride.

THE CASITA

en years had passed and the shaman had finally managed to find a house near the place where he had had his vision; that which had permitted him to know with certainty what God wanted from him and what he wanted from God. God wanted what he wanted and he wanted what God wanted.

The doors opened before him and the people of his blue family, his apprentices, began what would be a pilgrimage to the sanctuary that was being created in the house and the party atmosphere that was created there when they met together.

During the first year the members of the family that came to help him cleaned the house and took advantage of the opportunity to clean their personal life and their karma at the same time···

There was a lot of day to day work, and the shaman found himself finally at the door of his destiny: creating a new concept, a 'perceptual' revolution that would allow those who approached their apprenticeship to have a more relaxed and fruitful life. He was trying to create a concept where learning and being happy were identical.

"Life is hard enough without making it harder," he thought.

The dream took form little by little. He wanted to create a 'shamanastery': a shamanic monastery where apprenticeship, service, joy and love for life went hand in hand on the marvellous voyage of navigating in the mystery.

In the morning the apprentices did exercises involving movement of energy, whether it be chi-kung, or a shamanic method called fluidity. Afterwards, there was a healing session for those who came looking for the shaman as healer. Then, until lunch time, they fulfilled some service, which each carried out according to his inclination, either caring for, cleaning or improving the house, gardens or woods. The afternoon was dedicated to apprenticeship and at night there were drumming parties, inipis, meetings in the tipi or story telling sessions, amongst other activities involving entertainment and companionship.

Plenitude danced around the house and the apprentices to shamanism little by little learnt to court it, hunt it and let it manifest in their lives.

The house was set in the sacred mountains and was surrounded by forests of pine, ilex and oak, as well as cultivated fields of wheat and alfalfa.

Both the sanctuary and the house seemed to be isolated from the world without being so, which made them perfect for shamanic apprenticeship.

The conversations went on⋯

"Chamanito, speak to us about our destiny," asked José, an Andalusian builder who had come on holiday with his wife and daughters, one morning as they were hauling stones.

"Destiny is one of the most beautiful gifts that Spirit has given us. When we are born we come with a destiny and karma. Spirit gives you the opportunity of changing your destiny at your pleasure and convenience. You always have the opportunity of changing it and creating anew, but only apprentices to shamanism give themselves over to the task and pay the price of freedom.

The shaman takes and demands his cosmic right to change his destiny to his taste and to the taste of the Great Spirit. For this you need a lot of personal power, as well as a great capacity to call on the Great Mother Creator of the Universe and explain to her why and how you are going to change your destiny.

You need to know clearly what is the highest point you aspire to as a mortal, what is your biggest dream in the world.

Mediocre people don't have access to this possibility of changing their destiny. They live their life according to circumstances and it is circumstances that move their destiny.

The shaman's apprentice aims to change his destiny, and for this he needs the myth of the warrior or the myth of the shaman woman. He dares to move the Universe to change his destiny."

Luisa, José's partner, who had come over to bring them some water, asked on hearing the conversation, "What is the myth of the shaman?"

"Within your apprenticeship, you change yourself little by little into a myth. The mythological persons of humanity are always men or women who aspire and manage to go beyond the parameters of their social order.

The myth leads us to unfold the wings of our imagination and fantasy. In this way, our higher self can enter our subconscious and speak to our consciousness without putting our reason in danger. Reason doesn't feel threatened by the myth, because one of the functions of the myth is to balance reason with the magical side of life.

You can see the myth that you and your family are living: a normal woman and a normal man entering as a family into the search for knowledge, with beneficial results for the whole family and its structural stability.

Last night, in the gathering by the fire, you yourself embodied the myth: half housewife, half woman warrior; half jaguar, half human. Your eyes changed and your soul did too. Dancing around the fire you became other, the best of you came out. The myth has rescued your brilliance and, little by little, you are learning how to put it into your personal world. You feel fulfilled and full of confidence. You are living the myth of the middle-class woman who breaks through her social barriers and lives the life she always wanted to live, and you are doing this without putting your family's stability in danger. This is the best of the myth: you can live in both sides of reality. That is, you can be the woman who is half mystical woman and half everyday woman, a social triumph and a spiritual triumph.

Look at your daughters, healthy and happy. At some point you both made a promise to Spirit to have a happy family and you have fulfilled it, for this reason Spirit looks after you so well.

Luisa's eyes filled with tears and José looked up at the clouds that gave way to the light of the summer sun. His eyes seemed to speak to God and give thanks.

"What is the price of freedom?" asked Laura, an English woman who was travelling in Spain.

"The price of freedom, and therefore of changing your own destiny and having access to the life that you have always wanted to live, is the price of being happy. It is expensive, but payable. It consists of:

Stopping criticizing yourself.

Stopping criticizing others, whether it is in a constructive or destructive way.

Stopping seeing problems where there are no problems.

Stopping resolving imaginary problems and beginning to resolve concrete problems.

The price of happiness is renouncing thinking rubbish and stopping feeling things that aren't worthwhile.

The price of having enough energy to change your destiny is knowing how to look after the people that you love and knowing how to distance yourself from the people who are harmful to your energy.

The price of changing your destiny is daring to think about what it is that you have always wanted to do in the world and giving yourself the mental opportunity to believe that it is right and possible to achieve it.

The price of changing your destiny is trusting yourself although everyone doubts; not asking for advice and daring to act.

The price of changing your destiny is to give up "No···", "I don't know···", "But···", "I'm not sure···", "I don't know if I'm ready···", or any other of those mental stimuli that only lead you to sabotage yourself.

The price that you pay is stopping believing lying lies and beginning to tell yourself truthful lies.

As you see the price is high but payable. For it you need to cultivate discipline, impeccability, respect and discretion.

"What are lying lies?" asked Hilda, in her English accent.

"To re-establish your confidence in yourself you have to change your mental archives and your way of thinking about yourself. A lying lie is, for example, an archive that contains things your parents constantly told you, like 'you can't', 'don't be stupid', 'that isn't done', 'good girls don't do those things', or other negative sentences. This creates lying lies in your mind. 'I can't··· I haven't got confidence in myself, I don't like my body, I'm not attractive, nobody understands me.' When one repeats a lie many times, it ends up becoming the truth.

If you repeat to yourself every day 'I can't···', you will never be able to.

If you repeat, 'I'm not ready' you never will be···

"I understand that," said Hilda, "But have I really got to trick myself and live deceiving myself?"

"Of course, if that is what is in your interests so that you can be a happy woman. You 'deceive' yourself with beautiful truths. At the beginning, for you they will be lies, truthful lies.

Repeat 100 times a day 'I can achieve my objectives', and you affirm it as if it were the truth. Then you will discover that in one year you will convert this lie into an absolute truth.

Repeat every day 'I want to, I can, I deserve to··· be happy···' or whatever you want."

"But··· I don't know if I deserve to be happy," said Hilda looking at the floor.

"That is a lying lie," clarified the shaman, and he added, "Repeat 100 times a day:

'I am a woman who deserves the best of my world'.

'Every day it is easier and easier for me to take the best of what the world gives me'.

Or repeat these truthful lies:

'Every day I feel better, better, better'. Twenty times

before you go to sleep and twenty times on waking up.

It is important that you use positive terms, for example:

'Every day I am stronger', 'every day I have more free energy to be happy', 'with every day that passes I am more beautiful'···

'I like my legs, I like my body, I like my smile···'

'From today on I have greater capacity for triumph; from today on it is easier and easier to have confidence in myself; every day that passes I have more confidence in myself; every day that passes I feel happier with my life···'

'I want economic stability, I deserve economic stability, I am going to have magnificent economic stability···'

Always in present/future:

'Every day I gain more and more confidence in myself'

Always positive. Never say 'I no longer get depressed', say 'Every day I am more and more happy'.

Here is where you take the first step towards having quality thoughts."

"But I'm going to have to spend all day trying to say these sentences···" Hilda complained.

Faced with Agustín's confirmation, she added, "I don't know if I'll be able to."

To the shaman that looked like an opportune example of a 'lying lie', and he invited her to repeat affirmations such as 'every day it is easier and easier for me to be disciplined in saying truthful lies', and to look at herself in a mirror for a minimum of ten minutes, and repeat to herself a series of positive sentences about her physical appearance.

"It doesn't matter if you don't believe them," he reassured her, "Because through so much repetition it is possible to convert them into reality."

Hilda went off with the shine of triumph in her eyes. She knew that it wasn't going to be easy but that she would manage it.

"But I want to solve my problems," commented Karen, Hilda's friend.

"Yes," answered Agustín, and he thought for a long time before answering her. "Problems··· You have to learn to distinguish between real problems and imaginary problems, to learn to distinguish between your problems and the problems of others. The shaman's apprentice doesn't look for solutions to problems. He knows that problems will come to him.

Trying to solve problems is to involve yourself in problems. Problems are like getting stuck in mud: it's difficult to get out with clean hands. You carry around problems that aren't yours because you are good. Problems that don't belong to you are nothing to do with you; they decimate your energy and you can't solve them. Then··· you get worried.

Worrying about problems that aren't yours and which you can do nothing about creates intense wear on your energy and density in your aura. For you loving someone is worrying about them. Therefore you see their problems so that you can worry about them, even thought the majority are fictitious. For you and the majority of people, worry is a synonym for love. 'Because I love you, I worry about you.'

Worrying is only the fruit of the thoughts of your mind that create anguish. Thinking about someone with problems doesn't help them to solve them. Help has to be manifested in real concrete acts, not in thoughts. Perhaps in words of support. You can help, that is our work. We are here to serve, as long as the problem is real and the person wants or asks for help.

The shaman doesn't worry about his loved ones; he takes care of his loved ones. He doesn't fill the people he loves with imaginary problems and he isn't an accomplice to their weaknesses. Neither does he see himself as Don Quixote of La Mancha, looking for someone to help, because then we end up creating problems where before there were none."

The shaman looked at Karen, and told her: "I see you according to your virtues, not according to your defects or your problems. I don't weigh you down with my thoughts and when you have a real problem and I can't do anything real to help you with it, I carefully choose to think that you will resolve your inconveniences in the best way possible. Then I feel that it is only a small inconvenience that life has placed before you so that you can learn something and that you will resolve it quickly.

Life isn't easy. But we live in a marvellous world. Problems are there, stalking us, and we have to be ready so they don't trap us."

"Shaman, speak to us about gratitude," asked Maribel.

"My life is Service and continuous thanking of the Great Spirit for the beautiful things that I have received in this life. Although it isn't easy, my life is beautiful. So much so that I feel envy of my own life and I try to find the best way to thank the world and life for everything that it has given me.

You yourself have had a good life. You have lived a little of everything, and eighty percent of your existence is good moments or exquisite moments, while only twenty percent of your life has been a disaster. How will you thank those that have looked after you, supported you and given you beautiful moments in your life? The shaman's apprentice looks for the most beautiful way of giving thanks. He searches for ingenious and stupendous ways to show gratitude.

Look at this."

Agustín got out a compact disc from his rucksack. His eyes sparkled.

"Look, Maribel, I composed this music to give thanks to these mountains, to my apprentices. This music is for those people who were with me, enlarging their souls with my knowledge.

This music gives thanks to the woman who I loved and yet to whom I couldn't show how much I loved her. This music gives thanks to these beautiful years and the spirits of these mountains that have sheltered me and have nourished my soul.

I want to give my thanks to La Plana through impeccability, joy and music. In the shamanic world thankfulness is indispensable and it is our obligation to find beautiful ways to express and share what we have received in this apprenticeship."

"What about the woman that you love?" asked Maribel shyly.

"I don't want to die with out being able to express my thanks for the love I have for her. I don't want to die without showing her the intensity of my feelings. My love won't lead

92

me to seeing her again, but it leads me to knowing how to thank her for what she did to my soul. I don't want to die without her knowing.

It would be beautiful to see her again, but it was more beautiful meeting her. This demonstration of my love is my way of saying thanks."

Maribel looked at the cd and laughed aloud. The cover of the album said: 'Shamanic Vanguard: Shaman Blues'.

The days passed peaceably in what we now called the Casita. It was like a bubble suspended in time. Each of the people living in the house knew what it was they had to do and the shaman, as the head of the house, looked after everyone who was there.

"I wouldn't be the leader of my people," he told Friedgard, an Austrian pupil, "if I told my warriors, my shamanic apprentices, what to do with their lives.

I'm not the chief of my people so that they obey me or listen to me. I fulfil the same functions as the rest, and in addition I have to look after the security and well-being of everyone. Being chief means working harder towards the care for these people I love."

"But you work too hard and you don't look after yourself enough," said Friedgard.

"One day I will rest enough: the shaman has time to rest but not to be lazy. I have a lot to do and very little time in my life. I know that Death is observing me in the same way that I am observing Death. One day it will jump at me and I will look at it satisfied because I will have fulfilled my commitments in this life. Right now I can't die, but Death is stalking me. I don't have enough time in this short life."

"Agustín, speak to us about service," asked Kalyani, an English woman living in Granada.

"As living beings and apprentices to shamanism we come into the world to learn and to soak up life. As shamans we are in service to God, to humanity and to this beautiful planet. As shamans we have come not only to receive the best of the world, but also to give the best of ourselves. We come to serve, not to sacrifice ourselves, nor to be anybody's servant.

We are here and we train ourselves to serve those people who approach us. We support them in their best intention without becoming accomplices to their weaknesses. We support their virtues and we don't criticize their defects.

Spirit recruited us to extend the light side of reality. The force is with us. We are in service, but being in service doesn't mean sacrificing ourselves for anything or anyone.

I give the best of myself and I serve, but I don't sacrifice myself for anything. Spirit has never asked sacrifices of me; I have been asked for discipline and rectitude.

Our way of serving obliges us to be as honest as possible with ourselves and this rectitude is personal, in agreement with our pacts with Spirit.

Few things give me as much satisfaction as serving, but I do it from harmony, beauty, congruence and love for God.

Life is not always easy for the shaman."

Richard, who had worked with the shaman together with his wife Garbi, sent a letter to the entire group of people who had shared courses and meetings with him in an attack of jealousy. In it he threw out very strong criticisms about the man who had been his teacher, inventing anything that might appear to be true.

"Sometimes," Agustín said to Montse Sobrina, "we have to experience public dismissal. The Nagual spoke about being prepared for the day that someone speaks badly of us in public and it is then when we have to have the integrity and the strength to be indifferent. If what they say is true, then why am I worried? And if it is false, why should it bother me?

I can't let gossip destroy my peace. Nothing that this man can do will affect my desire to help humanity. He has to carry the responsibility for his feelings and his acts, and I can only be impeccable.

He gives me what he has in his heart: his anger. And I have to give him what I have in mine: a real desire that he and his partner should be happy and that he can use his own knowledge to improve the life of them both more and more. Everything we do in this life is written in eternity.

He has anger in his heart and he is trying to find someone to blame. Perhaps my indifference is a way of helping him. He will have to live the rest of his life with this load; I'm not going to make it heavier for him, I'm not going to drag him down with my thoughts."

"But Agustín," said Montse worriedly, "people will read that letter and some may believe that what he says is true⋯"

"Those that know me and know my heart, won't believe it⋯ They'll know that I have never lacked respect, neither for him, nor for Spirit. They will know that he is a man in a process of change; he is jealous and is looking for someone to blame. It was he who brought his wife here, and motivated her to follow the path of the shaman. And in this way he managed to help her grow and find the knowledge that he had always searched for.

Those that know me and have walked with me know my rectitude. I don't have to defend my image. If someone loses the path with a heart because of the gossip of a neighbour, or loses their family because they believe lies, or invent falsehoods, they will regret it all their life and that is their responsibility. Losing a loved one because of a lie, a piece of gossip or a thought about something that never existed except in their mind, is a very sad aspect of the human condition.

Each of us is responsible for believing in what we see, hear or think. I am responsible for my destiny and my destiny has brought me this lesson. My impeccability leads me to get the best out of the situation and learn what I have to learn. Not everything that people tell you is true. Not everything you read is true. Not everything you think is true. Not everything you believe you are looking at is true.

I tell you: don't believe what I say, just because I say it, look at the world and discover whether it is true or not. Question it and corroborate it."

"But Agustín, doesn't it make you sad?" insisted Montse.

"It's not the first time that I've seen something like this happen and, when it is close to me, it makes me want to cry. Yes it's sad, very sad, that the dark side of reality manages to infiltrate into human pettiness and leave its seed in the darkest part of us. Being honest before God is a true feat; and being honest before ourselves is harder still.

Many walk along this path of beauty, but few survive the blows of the dark side of reality. Each of us is the only one responsible for offering, or not, a feast to the predators of consciousness. My responsibility is to protect myself from the dark side of reality and the energetic vampires."

"What are energetic vampires?" asked Cliodhana, an Irish fiddler who was staying in the house.

"Energetic vampires are those people who, on approaching you, decimate your energy, whether to feed from it or simply to absorb it. They are those people whose contact wears your luminosity.

Energetic vampires have many types of personalities. You yourself are often one, and I.

There are depressive vampires who feed off the energy that is generated when you feel sorry for them. They are the ones that use sentences of the type '···only you can understand me···', '···you are my only friend, I can only trust you···', '···only you can help me with your advice···', even though they almost never follow your recommendations.

There are aggressive vampires: people, who through words or physical acts, intimidate your personality, decimate your energy.

Or questioning vampires, who are continually asking, without any real interest in the answer.

Or critical vampires, it doesn't matter what you do; they'll find a way to criticize you and decimate your self-esteem. It doesn't matter whether it is constructive or destructive criticism.

Or vampires that talk too much. You get sleepy when you are with them, but you wake up once you move away.

Or vampires that are always right.

Or vampires that beg for love: want me, love me, hit me but don't leave me. They want to oblige you to love them.

Or good vampires, those who impose their beliefs about what is good for you without asking you whether you want help.

Energetic vampires are normal, everyday people and you

give them all the power they have over you. They're not bad;
they're just dangerous. And you have the obligation to defend
yourself from them without causing them harm or offending
them with any rudeness."

BOOK TWO

Book Two

MEMORIES STOLEN
FROM THE DEAD STARS

he Casita had a little lake that the shaman and his apprentices wanted to convert into a place with Zen aesthetics, a place of contemplation, of beauty. The shaman was next to this lake accompanied by a group formed of his six most beloved apprentices: Petra, Verena, Manolito (Luís), Luís Toc Toc, Joanna and Christopher Robinson.

"I think this is the moment for you to read this," he told them, "'The Book of the Memories Stolen from the Dead Stars'.

I, Itzcoatl Papalotzin (Obsidian Butterfly Snake), I, Agustín, am sharing with you the book of knowledge that I have hunted and trapped in my dreams. I think this is the time to part with it and not have only my eyes reading it. I have written it in the same way as I have motivated you to elaborate your own.

For years, on waking up, I have written a sentence, a sentence that summarizes what I have been taught in my dreams.

There are days when the sentences say nothing, other days the sentences are memories of something I've read, or that the Great Mother Creator of the Universe has dictated to me, word by word, to open my eyes to her knowledge. There are days when the sentences are memories that I have stolen from the dead stars when, in my dreaming body, I have travelled through the mystery.

This book is the compendium of what I have learnt in my dreams.

You can't read it in a linear way; read it bit by bit, a sentence, a page, a concept. Don't try to read it from beginning to end. Jump pages and let the book read to you, let it decide where you should read.

For the last three years I have motivated you to write when you get up in the morning, without worrying about the content. Bit by bit, within your writings, you yourselves will discover a compendium of wisdom, formed by correct and substantial sentences. Today I want to share with you what I have found in the dead stars, that aren't really dead. This knowledge has been guarded and now it is time for it to begin its pilgrimage through this sacred planet. Part of this knowledge comes from the star that holds our cosmic origins."

With great respect, each of the apprentices took the photocopies the shaman had bound with covers of leather, and they all went to sit down and read the words of Agustín. In them they recognized their own memories, that at some time they too had stolen from the dead stars, and which now they remembered completely.

THE SOURCE

At the source
Energy was feminine,
And bit by bit the Great Mother
Created expansive energy:
Overwhelming
And devastating
Masculine energy,
Creating a mutation in consciousness,
Creating yin and yang,
Masculine and feminine,
Good and bad,
The dark side and the light side of reality.

In the beginning light moved
Through the black mass of the Universe,
Creating confusion where confusion hadn't existed.

In this feminine universe in expansion
There existed intense points of light
Where masculine energy dominated.
In those spaces of creativity
There exist filaments of light
Conscious of themselves.
They try to balance
Their masculine side with their feminine side,
Creating a consciousness unusual for its beauty
And for the quality of its consciousness.

In its origins, this place called Gaia

Was a point of pilgrimage
For those feminine consciousnesses
That wanted to balance themselves
With masculine consciousness.
This place called Gaia was dense and predatory,
But of an unusual beauty.

There were few feminine consciousnesses that
Fulfilled their task.
Therefore the Mother Creator of the universe
Gave them as a gift
The ability to try as often as they wanted,
Paying the energetic cost that each attempt required
In each reincarnation.

The Great Mother was touched
By the feminine search
For balance with this new masculine energy;
Acting with respect
She allowed things to take their course.

The planet Gaia
Could shelter different forms of consciousness.
The most peculiar, for its complexity
And interest in everything,
Was the human race.

At the beginning of creation
The universe was feminine.

And the filaments of light,
For mutual support,
Created lineages according to their colour
And their aspirations.

THE MYTH
OF THE BLUE LINEAGE

"The Universe is full of forms of consciousness,
And each consciousness has a Universe of manifestations.
The Universe is fed by the movement generated by
consciousness,
And by an energy called love."

The book of *'Memories Stolen from the Dead Stars'*

y name is Mokey and my first birth occurred on a small red star at the outermost point of our Universe. Of all the universes known to the forms of consciousness from my planet, this universe where we live is the darkest and most predatory, but it is also the only one that has that type of energy known as love. This energy nourishes our cosmos, everything that exists, existed, or will exist in our Universe.

Mine is a small planet that, looking in a straight line from the Earth, can be found in the direction of the Pleiades. It never occurred to its inhabitants to give it a name. My beautiful, small planet reached its end one day; it exploded and launched its remains throughout the known Universe.

Those that spoke with the heart of the star that gave us light said that our planet exploded in its attempt to change its consciousness, so as to enter distant universes and in this way become a Sun. However it didn't have enough energy, nor the lightness to achieve it, because it loved the conscious beings

105

that inhabited it too much, and it didn't want to go without giving them the opportunity to achieve freedom too, if they wanted. So it left us a map in our own luminosity.

My original form was like a small bubble of blue light, perfectly drawn, as if cut by a knife. Within there were filaments of light that looked like two feathers meeting. As we didn't have a physical body, we enjoyed great lightness and we were nourished by the light that emanated from our star.

Periodically we had to move our bubble of light, so we had to die, but we kept a part of our consciousness, which meant that we could remember part of our earlier life. This gave us an exquisite continuity, and enriched our love for life, because of its knowledge and its mysteries.

The destruction of our planet left us roaming the Universe - my race, my people, my tribe, my clan, my family and me. This wandering left us at the mercy of the predators of consciousness, of energetic masses from other universes, of the intergalactic vampires that gnaw at our luminosity.

Because moving through the Universe in groups kept them relatively distant, we never gave them much importance, a mistake we would pay for dearly some few thousand years later.

Roaming, we had to decipher the map that our planet had left us, and that is how our pilgrimage began.

We had to reach a doorway, an energetic trampoline, from where we could jump and return to our destroyed world, or to the understanding of the destruction and change of our planet.

In our understanding, the dead stars aren't really dead, but we didn't know where they were and, according to the map that our world had left us, the only place we could jump from was the third planet of a solar system, called 'Earth'.

This insignificant but beautiful planet was a point where three universes converged: a universe of love (the most subtle energy of the universe), another of predators (incomprehensible but observable, that gnaw the energy of the consciousnesses of the Earth) and another of organic beings (rich in both movement and opportunities).

This last was the world that presented the best opportunities for returning to what we called our home, or the last frontier. But this last universe was extremely dense, so dense that it made it practically impossible to fly.

In its turn, this density was what would permit us to take advantage of the lightness of our past to cross the last frontier.

Before reaching this planet we had to pass through and live some lives in other worlds. First we passed through a small, dark world near the constellations of Andromeda and the Corona Boreal, finally to jump through another planet that is over there, in Orion's belt.

On the Earth more than two consciousnesses live at the same time and in the same space, in the same coordinates of the cosmos.

> *"There are worlds and 'antiworlds'*
> *People and 'antipeople'*
> *Consciousnesses and 'anticonsciousnesses'."*

Although they occupy the same space/time coordinates, they rarely become conscious of the respective existence of each other, in spite of being able to witness each other continually.

One consciousness can pass through two spaces at the same time and not know it. This possibility, of being in two places at the same time, was one of the reasons why we decided to be born into this world of wonders.

Once on the Earth, at first we took forms without a body - Fairies, Dwarfs, Elves - and in these forms we were especially happy. But our love for our world led us to incarnate in the form that would allow us to return to our origins, one of the organic manifestations... the human being.

107

There is a big difference between being a human and being a conscious bubble of light. The human tends to forget earlier lives almost completely, which makes it much more difficult for us to remember our task. Then we can become trapped in an interminable vicious circle, as we have to keep incarnating until reaching illumination, or complete understanding.

We, in our original configuration as a bubble of light, could remember at least half our past experience. With the loss of this capacity we forgot our cosmic objective and we became limited to primary states: food, partner, reproduction and territoriality. So incarnating became a difficult task, and on top of this we had to battle with the predators of consciousness. But it was essential for our search that we go through it.

And that is where this story begins, with everything that I had to live through to be able to remember what I am telling you.

THE INTERPRETATION OF BIRTH

It doesn't matter in what universe
You exist, everything is an interpretation.
There are no good interpretations
Nor bad interpretations,
There are only useful interpretations
Or useless interpretations.

From the book of *'Memories Stolen from the Dead Stars'*

BEFORE BEING BORN

There is a place in the universe that seems to be made of ice and light and it is there where consciousness takes the human form and goes down to the world of incarnated beings.

I was one of the youngest consciousnesses of my world when it exploded, which made me especially sensitive to change. I was nervous about going back down again, in the process of reincarnation, to the planet Earth, in the human condition.

"You'll regret it," the old man told me.

I was scared in spite of feeling prepared. His words were not helpful.

"Maybe I should wait before going down. The last time I went I didn't exactly have a very good time," I said with a note of doubt in my voice.

"The universe will never give you a test without you having what you need to face it," the old man told me.

I knew he was right.

"And now, what is it that I should 'be'?" I asked, only for the sake of speaking. I knew very well that this time I would be male, a rare condition in the Universe, as this Universe is feminine, as opposed to that of the predators, which is masculine.

The old man didn't answer me and, taking me amiably by the hands, took me to a large space that looked like an enormous lake of ice, with a tone of silver and an agreeable, almost somniferous, heat.

"What is your choice?"

He was referring to the order of the doors through which I would pass.

There were four circular tunnels through which you could descend to the Earth. I looked at the first. That was the doorway for those who didn't want to be born. I had passed through that one and I knew that when you entered from there you didn't exactly have a good time.

The second was for those who want to have new experiences. Through it I saw a lot of old souls pass, but that wasn't the one for me this time, and I said so.

The next two were the ones that were for me. In one of them I would meet up again with consciousnesses that I had interacted with in other moments of my past lives: old mothers or fathers, brothers and sisters, children, teachers, pupils, or old loves.

And the last door, the one for those who have a task in the world, offers a symbolic payment to the world for occupying a space and the opportunity of life. It is the door of power, of influence in the world, and through it you can simply change the cycle of events. After fulfilling this task, you are free to cross the frontier, our most desired objective.

"Doesn't it move you when you see that there can be so many events, and that in that world things change so fast?"

He was referring to the speed of events, the rhythm of time and the limit of life of the organic beings.

"So it is, father," I told him while I embraced him with great love, "That's what makes it so wonderful," I said, while my eyes moistened with love for him.

"Do you know what your choice is now?" he asked me again.

"Yes, a middle class couple in Mexico City, six living children and two dead."

"And your conception?"

I looked down; I knew that I would not be conceived in a state of passion or orgasm on my mother's part.

"My mother will be in a state of madness because of the loss of two children before my conception. She will only be slightly excited physically, but there will be great desire for me to be born and, although I won't be born with a lot of energy, my energy will be of good quality."

The old man, who they called Father Rantu, worked out a general plan with me about what my life would be, advising me on very few occasions and respecting each of my choices. At some points I could just see a tear of worry that came out of his eyes. He was in agreement with each of my choices.

"Father Rantu! The predators? Do you know if there will be many in my destiny?"

We were walking through an area of violet light and he stopped his gentle walk, looked at me with his deep eyes, and said: "There will be as many around you as there are stars in the sky, and to battle with them you will have to put a series of strategies into practice. Congruence will be your best ally."

And, as he spoke, he handed me a small angel made of maize, the leaves of an ear of corn that enclosed two documents. One was a codex made on maté paper and the other some pages of computer printout. Something seemed out of place. "Are there computers in this place?" I asked myself mentally.

"Everything is an interpretation," he answered, reading my thoughts. "We have the obligation to adapt ourselves to the 'perceptual' vibration of the time to which we descend. The two books contain the same knowledge. They are the keys to remembering, and they are what will allow you to follow the map of return to our home," he explained.

"Everything that is in these sacred books is only a map. Only a map," he insisted. "But if you defeat the predators of consciousness, the lords of the dark side of reality, if you manage to distance them and recover the map, you will be able to reunite with those of your clan that go before you, and collect those that go after you, and then your task on this planet will be completed..."

One of the sensations I always had when I incarnated was that there was a group before me and I had to catch up with them.

We arrived at the third door, an enormous hole, through which thousands of souls descended daily, but we were alone. Birth is an individual matter.

"Are you sure that you want to go down?" he asked me again with a very soft voice.

"When will you go down?" I asked him by way of answer.

"When the last of my clan has found the path," he answered.

I felt a great desire to go down, to see the Sun again, to fight to cross the frontier; to meet again with a lot of loved ones. I knew that I wanted to arrive, that there was no sense in putting off my destiny any longer.

"The moment has finally arrived," the old man said in his gentle voice.

I nodded.

"Take this, so that you remember me," he said, stretching out his hand.

In it there was a tiny bubble of blue light. I took it and placed it in the centre of my luminosity. It was a beautiful memento. He had one the same; I embraced him and the two spheres united. I cried on separating from him. Great sadness inundated my heart while I descended through the long deep tunnel of light, but, but by bit, the sadness gave way to a profound desire to be born.

I didn't look at him to say goodbye, I just jumped within and violet light enveloped me. I reached a place where there was a flight of silver stairs. There I could hear my mother's heartbeat, my father's voice, the laughter of my brothers and sisters... Everything was truly beautiful; I could only perceive everyone's profound worry about me, in case I wasn't born. But that was now impossible; I had decided already.

In different but simultaneous times of my gestation I found myself both inside my mother and descending those stairs - a dual process. In this time of gestation I absorbed the indications contained in the maize angel that the old man had given me. I knew that I was going to need them in this life... I read the title of the written pages... Memories Stolen...

BIRTH

The first battle in life
Is against the predators of consciousness,
Who, on seeing you defenceless, divide your soul in two
So that you can't fulfil your task,
And they place you in two different places at the same time.

From the book of *'Memories Stolen from the Dead Stars'*

I longed be born, to leave my mother's womb, look at the loving face of my father, who harboured great expectations of my birth, of the possibility that through me my mother would recover her sanity. I wanted to feel the beauty of the first meeting again, the first ray of light, the leaving of the red world, which is what the womb is called, and arriving in the white world, multicolour. I wanted to breathe the air again and feel myself alive... I simply wanted to be born.

I went down the last steps, and a large sphere of light began to surround me, it was like a big space ship in which all my memories would remain. Below, life could be found. I had to jump, I wanted to live, to return to the battle, but I knew that in this jump I would have my first meeting with power... I would face the predators of consciousness... Without thinking about it much, I jumped.

Everything was dark. The predators surrounded me; they were simple shadows that moved from one side to another, they frightened me. Fear was my first mistake because all their power rests in this feeling. They know how to make you believe that it is you that is thinking, when really it is their thoughts projected within your mind.

"They will destroy you, hate them, get angry, they will make your life impossible," I heard in my ear. I knew that it was a predator who wanted to enter my consciousness.

"These thoughts aren't mine, out of me!" I told myself

113

with great decision.

"That's right!" I heard another voice saying, "they will never be able to do anything to you, your energy is much superior to that of any other entity, you can smash them or master them if you want to, because they are worthless."

"Of course!" I told myself when I realized that it was another predator who had said this. It had almost managed to trick me.

"Why do you want to be born?" said another voice. "You're going to suffer. Your father already warned you that you'd regret it."

"These are not my thoughts, I have no thoughts, out of me!" I began to shout desperately. I knew that I would be born any minute, I wanted to be born in a tranquil state, and they wouldn't let me.

"You will lose your loved ones again, don't you remember?" predicted another predator.

"You will lose your memories," insisted yet another.

"You won't know why you were born," said another, trying to confuse me.

"You will lose your connection to Spirit and it will be very difficult for you to re-establish it. It will be almost impossible," continued another, preparing along with the others never to leave me in peace.

The attack of the predators was tremendous and it touched every sensitive part of me. The only thing I had to do to be free was not to think, to simply recognize that those weren't my thoughts; that thoughts don't exist in the side of light where the power and freedom I aspire to are found. But they knew how to infiltrate and deceive.

Another tried to praise me to open a way into my consciousness.

"Don't think. You're going to be an important man in the world. You will be a great shaman, a holy man, you will have hundreds of pupils and they will love you so much."

The predators know how to play with truth and lies and, through the emotions they create, they manage to divide your soul.

"Don't think that it doesn't matter to you whether you are good or bad," said another predator.

I had almost reached the exit, but in the end I began to argue with them, with myself, and again my body split into two.

A wave of terror and pain began to split my soul in two, one half was being made prisoner by the predators. The silver part of me moved away with a soft smile of hope, and I, in anguish, began to cry, to beg, to ask my father to take me back to my world… to my inexistent home…

I heard the cry of a baby, my own cry, while I saw how a shadow carried away my other part, the silver part, that with a smile said, "return to me".

"It's a boy," said the doctor to my father.

My brother approached and took me in his arms. He shone in blue. It was the first time I saw light in a human being. I looked into his eyes and I knew that something in him understood. He was from my Clan. A wave of sadness enveloped me. This would be the mark of my birth, it was a pity, I was so keen to be born!

The old man was right; I would live to regret being born.

THE SECOND DEATH

I had reached a place where there was a silver circle; I recognized the colour. It was of the same luminosity as the place from I had left from in order to be born.

I entered the circle and I saw how, descending from the edge, in spirals or in straight lines, there were a large number of bubbles of light. Little by little these bubbles took on shape, and sat down on some type of stool. I could recognize some of them: those that were interpretations of Christian, Buddhist, Moslem or shamanic images, amongst other characters or wise people of the different cultures of the human world. All of the seats were filling up, but one remained empty and I knew that it was mine.

"All these manifestations of wisdom are those that have looked after you in different stages of your life Mokey," said the magical voice of Father Rantu.

It felt strange hearing my name. No one had used it since I was born on this planet.

The man that had called me by my name and who I called father the day of my birth, that time when I almost died on the mountain, got up from one of the chairs. I wanted to run and embrace him but I felt it wasn't the right moment.

"There will be another moment to express our love, young star," said Father Rantu affectionately.

"Why am I here?" I asked uncertainly.

In front of me an image appeared - it was Agustín, one of my existences, walking through the mountains of the Himalayas. He had gone on a pilgrimage to remember my cosmic origins and to redirect my destiny.

"Lord God," I heard the thoughts of Agustín as he walked, "I want to be your intermediary. The moment has arrived in which I shall become a doer of miracles. I want to touch the sick and cure them, I want to touch invalids and make them walk, I want my words to take pure understanding to the consciousness of my pupils and friends, I want to be on television and be famous, I want to be surrounded by beautiful women, I want to have many pupils and a lot of money, I want…"

I looked at my father. My look was charged with understanding, but also a little shame.

Bit by bit I lost energy. Walking through the mountains my vitality was converted into tiredness. I lost all my strength and in this way two days passed. Weakness had reached such an extreme that I had to go to my room and I could no longer manage to get out of bed. Pride had opened a mortal hole in my luminosity. The predators had fed off my energy for days, driving me to energetic haemorrhage and real death.

I saw a Buddhist monk enter together with one of my pupils who had accompanied me on this journey.

"It smells of illness in here," he said. "Go out and breathe pure air."

I didn't have energy to excuse my weakness, so I decided to do what he said and, after taking ten minutes to put on some shoes, and the same again to leave the room, I took a track that led away from the house where I was staying.

"Father, I have seen enough, I have understood," I said, "Can I return to the world?" I hoped that with these words the image would disappear, but that wasn't the case.

In answer another scene appeared in which I was stretched out on the mountainside, in my death agony. I had no energy either to move or speak. I only had energy left for thinking. I was dying with no real cause.

Two pheasants flew over my head and I mentally said goodbye to the world, understanding that my pride had given me a fatal blow and had broken my luminosity.

I saw how my soul left my body and was sucked through the circular tunnel of silver through which I had arrived at the conclave of the wise, where I now was.

"Your body," said my father, "is stretched out on the mountainside, 4,000 metres high, lifeless and with no one around who can rescue you. Your spells have left you without energy; you have wasted yourself by allowing yourself to be trapped by the predators of consciousness. Returning will be worse than staying here, because you will deny yourself the

117

occupation of the seat that is yours by right."

Everything seemed to be a game of Spirit. I said good-bye to each of the energies that were present, thanking them. I was in a hurry to return to my body, I needed to live. I couldn't allow myself the luxury of a stupid death.

I awoke stretched out on the ground. Now I could move and speak. My pupil finally found me and told me off because she had been very worried about me. Ten hours had passed since I had left my room. Listening to her speak felt absurd. I thought about the little I could remember of the place where I had been, I could barely recall a couple of minutes in the circle of light.I looked at her and saw her anger and, with no strength to argue, I let her take me to the house of the Tibetan Buddhist without saying anything.

In the night, alone in the room, I remembered...

"...So that your descent to the Earth is easier, from now on we will manifest ourselves and allow ourselves to be interpreted as human beings, not as bubbles of light. I will take on the role of father or wise protector with you as the son or youngest apprentice within our clan..."

"There are different clans or cycles, but each cycle has an objective..."

"And so that it will be easier for you to know your objective on the Earth, you will take with you this key that will give you access to the memories of the dead stars, you only need to rescue them, to steal them..."

THE THOUGHTS
OF THE STARS

nly in your dreams
Do you enter into the knowledge of the dead stars.
But to take it back to the world in the form of consciousness,
You must steal it,
Ask for it without permission;
But always with the respect that knowledge deserves.
Recognize that it belongs to you by right.
You have the right to take this precious jewel
For human consciousness.

The truly wise aren't wise;
The truly wise don't know that they are wise.
There is no good seer who proclaims that he is a seer,
But all his being knows that he is.

No one and nothing can take away your right to be free.
Freedom consists in taking it for yourself:
Nobody can give it to you.

There are different types of freedom:

119

Freedom to remember who you are.
Freedom to escape that which imprisons you
And distances you from your function in the universe.
Freedom to be conscious
And understand the universe in which you exist.
Freedom to decide to direct your life
And choose the manner of your death.
Freedom that gives you energy to expand your
consciousness,
And free yourself from whatever imprisons you.
And freedom to die carrying your consciousness with you,
And to continue your voyage through the cosmos.

To look for the path is to look for freedom,
But we have to know what it is we want to be free from.
What distances us from our fellow beings?
What obsesses our thoughts?
Or what makes peace and harmony
Two abstract terms?
What distances us from the freedom
To be able to be what we want to be?
What distances us from fulfilling our task in the world?

Having the freedom to
Love without fear, feel fear without fear, cry without
prejudice,
Enjoy sadness and allow yourself to flow with it.
Freedom to stop depression, criticism, jealousy,
Lies, those obsessive thoughts
We confuse with reality.
Freedom to stop all those thoughts that aren't
Ours, identifying the thoughts of Spirit, and
Freedom to be able to follow divine words.
Freedom to decide the path we want to live,
The job we want to have, the company we want,

The life we want to live.
Freedom to remember who we are,
Where we are, and where we come from.
Freedom to love our loved ones
Without social conditioning,
And without the lies of our predecessors.
Freedom to break those genetic archives,
That condition our race, our sex,
And our manner of death.
Freedom to stop our vices - physical, mental,
Emotional, to stop the vice of creating a reality
According to our thoughts and not according to reality.
Freedom to die in states of power
And to choose if we want to come back to the world again.
Freedom to be healthy and strong,
Full of energy and life.
Freedom to discover who feeds off your energy
And your consciousness.
And freedom to stop those losses of energy
And consciousness.

Just as you take knowledge,
So will someone or something take it from you.
Just as you take the energy of the cosmos
Something is taking energy from you.
In this universe there are
Predators of consciousness
Who feed off your energy.
The predators
Feed off your intensity,
Off your consciousness,
Off your thoughts.
They are like dark stains
That move about the floor.
They filter into your thoughts by means of two stings:

They speak through one and you believe they are your
thoughts,
And through the other they absorb the energy
You waste by thinking rubbish.
The predators feed off the dark side of your being.
You are their food and you didn't know it: you were free of
blame.
Now that you know it, it's not possible to avoid action.
The predators leave you just enough energy
To stay alive.
Few manage to shake them off.
Only discipline gets them out of your brain.
The predators of consciousness
Don't want you to know.
They won't allow you to steal
The memories of the dead stars,
Even though they are yours by right.

TESTS

Small tests
Always appear when we least expect them,
We are never warned that they are tests.
If you pass the test no one tells you,
So you don't waste your energy in feelings of triumph.
And if you fail they don't tell you either,
So you don't waste your energy in feelings of failure.
True tests appear
When your thoughts believe
That you're not ready to face them,
And you face them.
Those tests
Where you think you're ready
And you face them, are worthless.

Those that are worthwhile are those
That you feel you aren't ready for.
Spirit never gives you any test
That your energy is not ready for.

Nothing real can be threatened.
Nothing unreal exists.
Herein lies the peace of God.
(From "A Course in Miracles")

You invoke your direction, the change within the dream.
The greatest feat within dreams
Is to awake in the dream that you want to dream,
Awake in the life that you always wanted to live.
Waking in the dream of your choice
Is only the first step
To finding the doorway out.

Everything is a ramification of dreams,
Everything happens at the same time.

On beginning to defeat of the predators of consciousness
The soul discovers sadness and emptiness,
Not with the fear that the flyers gave,
But as tools and recognition of your advances.
The first great achievement
Is accepting emptiness in your soul
And sadness in your chest;
The longing of your consciousness
And the nostalgia of your wisdom.
Solitude permits you to be complete,
To become a friend to yourself.
You can be alone in the company of another
And still be complete.
You can be alone in your own company

And still be complete
Feeling good alone,
Not fearing solitude,
And with a man, a woman,
You can be alone
And feel complete.
Your solitude allows you company, to have a partner;
But your solitude is your solitude,
Your connection to the abstract,
To the other, to the dream body.
Only with her, can he recognize his feminine solitude.
Only with him, can she achieve recognition of her masculine
solitude.
When you become a friend of your solitude it doesn't matter
If your partner understands you.
Then you open the door to understanding.

There are men who have a feminine soul
And every woman has a masculine soul.
The masculine side of the being tries
To have confidence in her courage, although everyone
doubts,
And she triumphs.
The feminine side of the being tries
To govern herself.
Masculine energy gives direction,
Feminine energy gives reach.
This is called balance within solitude.
Only the wonder between man and woman makes us
human,
Because she is him and he is her.
The man tries to discover what a woman is.
The woman tries to discover what a man is.
They are like two different races that occupy the same
species.

They are like two different languages
That know how to communicate.
The man and woman have objectives in common.
This unites them in this feminine cosmos.
These objectives are reproduction,
The search for consciousness,
Balance
And communication.
When they discover each other
And recognize the immense difference
And learn to enter into the other,
Solitude disappears.
Then plenitude arrives.

The predators of consciousness
Don't want men to discover their feminine side,
Nor women to discover their masculine side:
They filter into your thoughts criticizing the opposite sex.

The woman is like a triangle
With the point facing down,
She sets off from the point and is projected into the infinite.

The man is like a triangle
With the point facing upwards,
He sets off from any point and has an objective,
But the point of the pyramid limits him.

What is difficult for a woman is not to project her,
It's to bring her back;
The woman is abstract by nature.

What is difficult with a man is to project him,
Break his shell
That limits him to his specific objective.

The woman, as she has a womb,
Has double the available energy of a man.

The everyday man,
Little by little steals confidence from the woman
And her self esteem, so that he can manipulate her.
The man manipulates everything through
Words and emotional blackmail.
The liberation of woman
Begins when she realizes that it is impossible
For the man to be always right,
And that his world is not balanced.

The shaman, with his partner, first seeks
For her to re-establish her self esteem,
And relocate her power in her centre, the womb.
The shaman helps woman to free
The energy of her womb.

The woman has a womb that is a second brain
And the nearest thing to God that man knows;
But the predators of consciousness
Have limited this second brain
To reproduction and sexual pleasure.

The man thinks with his head.
The Indian thinks with the heart.
The shaman thinks with the belly.
The woman thinks with the womb.

When the woman thinks with the head she becomes
confused:
When she learns to think with the womb,
Absolute certainty arrives.

126

To reach absolute certainty
And the knowledge of her power within the womb,
She must free herself of the energy
That men have left within her vagina,
And the energy left by the social order with respect to her
children.

Three voices exist within your mind:
The voice of seeing,
Which is absolute certainty and communicates softly and
slowly;
The voice of the predators,
Conscious masses that feed off your energy
And your consciousness,
And your personal voice. Your I,
That has the power to redirect your personal universe to the
Dark side or the light side of reality,
The place where consciousness is cultivated.

Your first stage of apprenticeship
Is learning to master these three minds,
Eliminate the voice of the predators of consciousness,
And break the states of alignment in which you live
As a normal everyday person.

Your personal universe is ruled by the power of the dark
side
That you feed and strengthen,
And the power of the light side, absolute consciousness,
Total freedom.

To fight the predators of consciousness
Discipline is necessary.
The discipline to not believe anything you tell yourself,

Neither the good
Nor the bad,
Nor to believe what they say about you.
Check every thought
And ask yourself:
Is this thought mine?
Do I want it?
If it isn't yours simply refuse to think it.
Throw out the thought.
Remove it from your mind.
The predator will search for another place
Where it can get at your energy.

What you see and live
You believe to be your experiences,
But in reality they belong to Spirit,
The Cosmos, to God, to the Great Mother Creator of the
Universe.
Your experiences don't belong to you.
For them to belong to you, you would need to have
Double awareness of them.
One for you
And another for Spirit.
The Universe is given direction by the consciousness
Of each and every living particle of the cosmos.
The predators steal this consciousness
And then they hand it over to the cosmos as their own
experiences.
The human is chained
To the cycle of having to relive these experiences
To hand them over to consciousness.
This is reincarnation and the cycles.

Good and bad
Are two primitive states of consciousness.

Friends are made
When there are problems.
Gratefulness is the best glue.
Friends exists when they exist
And go when they go.
Being a friend of a true man
Is a great honour.
Being the friend of a true woman
Is really a great privilege.
Few have the honour of looking after
A true being,
Of giving thanks
For the opportunity of having met them,
For the amount of true friends
We have access to.
Sometimes it isn't easy to cultivate
The best of ourselves in them,
We only support them in their best intention,
We don't criticize them
And we don't believe everything they say of us
When they are angry.
As a friend you learn to be
Indifferent to problems
And serene in solutions.
A true being,
A normal person
Should have as many friends
As stars in the sky,
But not all at the same time.

It is the conscious man
Who takes the apprentice under his protection,
Depending on what the apprentice has to offer
Humanity

Through his capacity and dedication
To each thing he does
In his personal world.

The apprentice, on making a commitment to
The abstract and to the shaman,
Agrees a period of earthly time
To awake beneath the shadow of the shaman.
In this time he establishes a relationship of knowledge
That is almost passionate.

The shadow of the shaman
Transforms everything.

The impeccability of the apprentice gives shape to his new
life.
The respect and admiration of the shadow
Is what gives aesthetics to the result.
Indifference and gratitude permit the apprentice
To leave the shadow and learn to give shelter himself.

Reason travels with whoever pays most.
Reason is an intellectual whore,
That goes with the highest bidder.

The most primitive love is called ambition.
You admire what you would like to have.
The shaman fights to separate the concepts
Of unconditional love and second-rate ambition.
The shaman strives after quality,
And he is terrified of second-rate ambition,
The sort that erodes, that imprisons you, that others dictate.
If you manage to find unconditional love
And you separate it from eroding ambition,
You will discover a new sea within you,

Vast and solitary,
Vast and wonderful.
Love is quality energy,
Which by itself achieves nothing.
You need certain, impeccable acts.
Impeccability is another quality energy.

The first law of love is
Don't believe you are in love.
The second law is
Never doubt that you are in love.
The third law of love is
Enjoy love to the maximum.
Love is like a ghost,
Everyone speaks of ghosts but few have direct experience.
Love is the basic energy of the universe,
But it isn't everything.
It is only one of the many ways
That Spirit manifests.
The shaman understands that love
Is just one more energy in the Universe,
But the most exquisite, abstract and desired by the human
being,
And also the scarcest.
The shaman glues everything he does with love,
Appealing always to impeccability.

The apprentice learns not to be humble.
He learns not to feel important.
He learns to be the best of himself.
An impeccable consciousness.

CONSCIOUSNESS

Consciousness is the tastiest fruit in the universe.
Consciousness and self-reflection
Are two different places.
Self-reflection is where
The predators of consciousness nest,
The fliers, energetic wear and tear.
Consciousness is the voice of seeing:
It is absolute certainty.
It is almost impossible to tell the difference:
One strengthens you and the other weakens.
Only consciousness and silence
Take you to the strength of the voice of seeing.

The predators of consciousness
Have many names:
Jealousy, fears, resentment, avarice,
Social order,
Arrogance, humiliation,
Feeling more than others,
Feeling special,
Devils, dwarves, chaneques, tulhu...

Another way of recognizing the predators of consciousness:
Compulsion.
Compulsion is simply obeying an order
Given by the predators of consciousness.
There is no consciousness, not even desire.

Constructive or destructive analysis is food for the
predators.
Self-reflection, hors d'oevres for the predators.
Egomania: banquet for the predators.
"But, but, but", indicates that the predators

Are feeding off you.
"No" is a way of accepting being food for the fliers.
Justification: dessert for the fliers.

There are forms of freedom
That allow us to understand that we don't want
To feed the predators of consciousness.
How to find ways of loving
That aren't food for them?

Who dares to love without feeding them?
Loving without suffering,
Without feeling jealousy,
Without getting depressed,
Without despairing the loss of the loved one,
Without justifying ourselves,
Making love something worthwhile.

How to love a loved one from the place of unconditional
love
And survive the predators of consciousness?
Why do they wait at every turn of the path
To jump us and feed off our gains,
Our misfortunes?
Who can dare to love from emptiness,
From sadness,
Recognizing longing
And getting carried away by nostalgia?
Who can dare to love from consciousness,
However frustrating and deceptive it seems?

Who dares to live a love that is worthwhile:
For a second
For a day
Only for a caress?

ORIGINS

Planet Earth is populated by two races:
The two form the human race.
Some are natives of the planet
And others are travellers in the universe.

The consciousness of some, the natives of the planet,
Was created in this same world.
That of the others comes from distant worlds.

Some are called young souls
And the others, ancient souls.

There is no physical difference:
They can be of the same race or the same family,
They can be brothers, and share the same blood:
The only difference is in the origin of their consciousness.

Before descending as human beings, the ancient souls
Pass through the kingdom of the fairies or elves,
Until they have the courage to incarnate as human beings.
Their great fear is that of knowing that they will lose almost
all their
Cosmic memory of their origins, and of the great weight of
the receptacle
Of their soul, the body.

Ancient souls always feel themselves to be in the wrong
place:
They always consider that they have another parent
Somewhere in the world,
They always have a gigantic desire to meet
With their people without knowing what this means.

Their chest shines with an ice blue and that is infinite
longing,
Sublime nostalgia and mortal sadness.
The feminine side of their ancient soul
Sometimes requires them to have children so as not to die.
There are ancient souls that remember
And ancient souls that don't remember;
Some are wise and have energy
And others exist in the chaos of forgetting.
The ancient souls know that the world is a dream.
And that is how they approach it.

The most important thing is energy
And after that, consciousness.

UNIVERSE

Everything in the universe converges
On a single point.
Every place is united with the Whole
By means of threads of light.

There are worlds and anti-worlds
Men and anti-men,
Light and shadow.
They occupy the same space and the same place
In time and in space;
They converge on a single point
In parallel universes,
And they are different consciousnesses.

There is a struggle in the human universe;
Two forces meet:
The predators of the universe

That inhabit the dark side of reality,
And the consciousness of the higher self
That inhabits the light side of reality.
The prize of this battle is our consciousness.

When two forces meet,
Either they harmonize
Or they fight.
When they fight both lose.
The apprentice urgently escapes this battle.
There is no prize for anyone,
Although the prize is consciousness,
The bubble is maltreated.

The apprentice seeks to be beyond good and bad.

One feels one is walking on a knife edge,
On one side is good,
On the other side is bad:
They are two dangerous abysses for the apprentice.

In the abyss of bad
Live those who have failed
In their search for freedom.
They systematically try to obstruct any other seeker
Or winner that they meet with on their path,
Because their success will always remind them of their own
failure.

In the ravine of bad live neurotics
Who don't live the life they want to live.

In the abyss of good
Exist those who have sacrificed themselves for others.
They don't live the life they would have liked to live either:

They are good people who aren't happy.
They constantly invade the intimacy of others
To step on them with their goodness,
Or their desire to help, looking for problems where none
exist.

They justify their need to be good
To be spiritual,
In order to hide all their deficiencies
And their promises of failure, of mediocrity,
Or their lack of capacity
To live a fulfilled and productive life.
They are born conquistadors:
Merciless when their goodness is not recognized,
And dangerous when you think differently to them.

The apprentice is very careful not to fall
Into either of these abysses and their sub-abysses.
Fighting to be beyond good and bad,
He has his shamanic code of impeccability
And love and respect for the world.

He is neither good nor bad,
Neither humble nor important,
But totally the opposite:
He is an impeccable being.

The Great Mother Creator of the Universe
Is the force that brings together
Consciousness and life:
She is the power that rules our destiny.
That which you call God,
I call the Great Mother Creator of the Universe.
But the Great Mother Creator is impersonal:
She is neither good nor bad,

She does no favours
Nor punishes anyone.
She simply obeys personal power
And its corresponding mandates.
All our work consists of
Cleaning our connections
To Her.
The Great Mother Creator of the Universe is called
By means of the shine in the eyes,
And the mandates are made
Through the energy of the womb,
Or two fingers width below the belly button.

Sexual energy
Has nothing to do with love.
Love is necessary for balance
And plenitude.
Sexual energy is necessary
For creation and passionate movement.

Plenitude, harmony and illumination
Are constructed of three energies:
Love
Impeccability
And consciousness.

The universe is full of lineages,
Human consciousness is full of lineages.
A world and a blue lineage exist for you.
The blue lineage is the most mysterious and solitary.
It isn't the best but it is what is offered to you,
It is what will lead you to the doorway out.
The consciousness of the blue lineage
Exists in the world only as a point of passage.
The Earth is the doorway,

The trampoline that gives the impulse to continue on the
path
Of return to cosmic origins,
To redirect destiny.

The price of the stay
And the opportunity of being in this marvellous world
Is your memories.
On being born you forget almost all your cosmic memories.

The blue lineage uses sadness
To lead to creativity;
Longing
To remember where it is going and who is waiting;
And nostalgia to remember its cosmic origins.
Only existential emptiness gives enough space
So that these three feelings
Are able to shape the true self:
The higher soul.

Only this emptiness allows the understanding
Of the memories stolen from the dead stars.
All these feelings of the soul,
All this emptiness,
Is wrapped in a blue sphere in the chest,
And this sphere is called plenitude.

We are in a predatory universe:
Someone wants to eat us
And we want to eat someone.
The prey that your consciousness seeks
Has to be the size
Of your cosmic origins,
The bigger and more extensive your prey,
The larger will be the memories that you discover.

All knowledge has a price,
Nothing is free,
Although we can take anything for free.

In this world two consciousnesses exist,
The living and the dead.
Not all those who are near you are living;
You are not always alive.
You will find people who seem to be real,
Who seem to be alive.
You may even fall in love with them,
But you will discover that they are ghosts
Created by the predators of consciousness
To distract your attention from the doorway out.
Recognizing that not all the people you know are alive
Or dreaming in some part of the universe,
Is the second doorway out.

Living beings have body and consistency;
They are conscious of the marvellous world in which they
exist
And they are conscious that they are going to die.
The dead live in the past
And think about the future.
They only see projections of their thoughts,
And they never discover what it is to live in the present.
Living in the future and the past
Is dangerous.
You run the risk of becoming trapped
In parallel, abstract dimensions.
It is poison.

The dead consciousnesses of the blue lineage
Are afraid to remember,

Because on remembering and confronting the time from the
present,
Everything they believe they know and everything they
believe they have
Loses consistency.
And then absolute emptiness descends to rescue them
And give them the opportunity to fill themselves with some-
thing worthwhile.

The price is high but it is payable.

The price of navigating in consciousness is high
And too absurd to be understood.
Part of the price to be paid
Is to abandon the rubbish of the social world:
Envy,
Unjustified anger,
Jealousy,
Resentment,
Unjustified fears,
Anxiety,
Mental masturbation,
Envy,
Among many other emotions.
The payment is to banish these thoughts from the mind:
Their uncontrolled impulses
And the feelings of wear that they provoke.

The voice of consciousness
Invites you to impeccability,
To discipline,
To find gifts in any situation,
To observe without judging,
To act rapidly and cautiously.
The voice of consciousness can be heard far off in the

beginning,
Behind all those voices and cries of the predators.
Bit by bit it takes strength and power:
The more power the voice of consciousness has,
The more peace your soul has.

The predators remove discipline and implant exigency.
Then you are cruel to yourself,
You mentally attack yourself,
And you insult yourself if you make a mistake.
You are mentally cruel when you are not what you want to
be,
You suffer because you are not what you want to be,
You suffer because the world is not as you would like it.
Exigency is to use the worst words you know against
yourself.
This process is one of the favourite and most common
Banquets of the predators of consciousness at your expense.

The voice of consciousness takes you to kindness,
To tolerance,
To unconcern,
And to impeccability.

To survive the battles with the predators of consciousness
Every apprentice cultivates
Unconcern,
Tolerance,
Discipline,
And the purest impeccability.

Even if an action is not important to him,
He acts as though it mattered
And he gives the best of himself.

Every human being seeks two things:
To be happy
And to distance himself from suffering.

Beating the predators of consciousness
Is the maximum achievement of an apprentice:
The most immense challenge for mental discipline,
And the basic requisite for becoming
A man of knowledge.

Each new sigh of consciousness
That a human being gives,
Is a hope of creativity for the Earth.
When the Earth dreams,
Consciousnesses dawn in the world.
Meditation leads to absolute silence.
There are different levels within silence.
On stopping the predators of consciousness
We identify which thoughts are ours
And which are not.

The thoughts of our progenitors,
Friends, loved ones and social system, which are not ours,
Come within our cultural or genetic patterns.
We learn to identify them and negate them if it is necessary.
We manipulate the information to create a reality
More to our taste and that allows us to
Harmonize our social world.
We learn to identify the thoughts
That belong to our personal interests,
We learn to identify them
And to channel our energy
Towards those thoughts.
We also call this consciousness or
Absolute consciousness.

You know what you want and how you want it,
And you have the capacity to programme and create
A strategy for achievement of goals.
These thoughts possess
Great discipline and great concentration.

The voice of seeing
Is like a voice that belongs to
Our higher self;
It gives us short convincing advice.
It doesn't explain, it only directs.

At first it seems
A distant voice,
Trapped in an uproar of thoughts,
Of different contexts.
The shaman's apprentice, on learning to silence the mind
And banish absurd and wearing thoughts,
Identifies the voice of seeing little by little.
This voice always has our best answer.
It is what we call our higher self.
It is the most highly evolved part that you have at your dis-
position.
From here comes absolute silence:
There are no words, there are no feelings.
It is a sensation we are not accustomed to,
Because it takes us to emptiness.
The bigger the emptiness,
The more distant the interpretation of the world that we
know.
We no longer interpret the world,
We only observe it from emptiness.
Everything that we believe in, that is not real,
Vanishes like tears in a storm.
Internal silence must be accompanied by energy.

We need immense doses of available energy
To give direction to the worlds of interpretation
And channelling of consciousness.
Internal silence without direction is only emptiness
In consciousness.
This emptiness is indispensable for the adequate channelling
of
Direction in this life.
This internal silence is accumulative.
The apprentice seeks
To accumulate many minutes of internal silence,
Identify them and later channel them.
The apprentice seeks transformation.
When he is in good shape he transforms to evolve.
When he is in bad shape he transforms to survive.
Emptiness is an energetic space
Where you can place
A new life.
The blue lineage belongs to the third millennium,
To the sixth sun, to the new humanity.
It carries the mark of the new era
And of the higher self.
Its members are the carriers of new knowledge
And a new family structure.

This knowledge carries
The stamp of balance,
Between feminine energy and masculine energy,
Between impeccability and indifference.
To be a blue apprentice
One needs a lot of respect
For life,
For the universe,
And for personal pacts with Spirit.

Navigating in the sea of consciousness
Has three prerequisites:
Discipline,
Consciousness,
And daring.
The apprenticeship of navigating in consciousness
And evading the limits of the social order
Is madness,
And only a few sane people
Can have the daring.
Navigating in the sea of consciousness is
The most beautiful and most solitary voyage there is.
It is only comparable to illumination and plenitude.

Plenitude,
Internal peace,
Indifference from a space of consciousness,
Illumination,
Are the keys to the door
That leads us to the space in the universe
Where all the answers are.
It is in this place that one reads the book
Of the dead stars.
There the Mother Creator of the Universe
Shelters us
And allows us to remember who we are,
Why we are,
What our gift to the world is
And where we are going.

The dead stars have left a map in our luminosity
And it is our pleasure and obligation to follow it.

The apprentices thumbed the document with gratitude and fascination. The lake seemed to contemplate them from its tranquillity and it contributed to the growing, contagious serenity of that dreaming place.

They knew that this gift was just another wink of Spirit, in whose service Agustín had placed himself so that they would always have a tangible reference to that magical situation, to that moment of plenitude that each one was experiencing, and to that universal feeling they were sharing: the feeling of connection to Spirit. The books were a magical gift, the beginning of a personal myth.

Of all of them, Manolito was the one who seemed most anxious.

"Agustín, is what is written in this book real?" he asked.

"Manolito, look around you," answered Agustín, "everything you see belongs to a dream. This book that you have read is real because you are dreaming it. In some place in the Universe, Manolito dreams that he meets the shaman he always wanted to meet and that he read the book that he always wanted to read. Everything that you are living is your dream and, because of a chance of destiny, your dream and mine met in a crossing of consciousness.

The answer is yes. Yes it is real, everything is a magical interpretation and there still remains a lot to dream and there still remains a lot for me to write."

"Agustín, what is going on?" asked Elizabeth, Agustín's mother and also an apprentice of his.

"Mama, look around you," insisted Agustín, "everything that you can see belongs to a dream. I brought this book from a dream. In some place in the Universe, your dreams became a myth, the same as the other apprentices. Even whoever is reading about us now may possibly become a myth. We have coincided in a dream and we are enriching the writing, enriching the myth, enriching the Universe with our experience, our friendship, with our unconditional love.

I am happy to have you here with me, but I am only a dream.

Look at this group of apprentices. They know that all this is a dream. They are ready to travel to where the stars keep their secrets. Soon I will be able to decide what to do with the second book.

But after, nothing will be the same."

The stolen memories have to be stolen,
And the dead stars are your accomplices;
They guide you and teach you
The tricks of their secrets.
You write without really knowing who writes.
And you read without knowing why you do it.
And finally you remember the sleeping place
Of he that dreams you,
He that writes,
He that led you to read this writing,
He that knows the stolen secrets,
He that speaks with the dead stars.

From the second book *of Memories Stolen form the Dead Stars*

BOOK THREE

SHAMANIC STRATEGIES

he shaman was having difficulty in finding a way in which the Europeans could understand his knowledge, as a large part of what he had learnt lacked relevance in Europe. He spoke about this at depth with four of his apprentices: Verena, Carmen Yoldi, Jesus de Mula and his wife, Paquy. He explained to them the obstacles to putting into suitable words the shamanic cosmovision he had inherited, and to developing apprenticeship methods for Europe.

His own process of apprenticeship had taken place half the time in cities, dealing with people, and the other half in nature, far from any urban centres. His teacher José had first led him to perceive and experience realities, and then afterwards to understand what had happened. In Europe things seemed to function in reverse: first the apprentices wanted to understand an experience and then they wanted to live it.

"I need you to learn to educate your mind and not let anyone steal the joy of living from you," he told Verena.

"Where does mental discipline lead us?" she asked.

"Let's see Verena, mental discipline leads you to a place where, when you are happy, no one can steal that pleasure from you. For the majority of people in the social world, their happiness depends on how others treat them.

For example, if your boss comes to your desk and throws something that you have written with great care on the table and tells you with a look of contempt on his face that it's no good, in that moment he steals your self esteem, your happiness and your pleasure in your work. He robs you of the well-being in which you were immersed. You end up mentally arguing with him, or justifying yourself, or feeling sorry for yourself, or simply his words and his look spoil your day.

To combat this you need a good strategy: what I call 'the four circles of action'."

"What are the four circles of action?" asked Carmen.

"The four circles of action constitute a basic strategy for looking after yourself within shamanism. We have a strategy, but we need to train the mind so that, when difficult circumstances arise, you are immune to the words, conduct or attitudes of the people who surround you. It is a strategy that isn't for everyone, but that works well.

The strategy consists of making a list of the 100 people who have most influenced or influence you in your world, who have the power to make you happy or to remove your happiness with a word or an act. The four circles of action to which I refer are those in which you place each of these people. Your list should also include your 'energetic vampires', who you will place in the third circle."

THE FOUR CIRCLES OF ACTION

FIRST CIRCLE OF ACTION

"Here you will only place those people who beautify, enrich or make your life a wonderful apprenticeship. These are your exquisite people and only they can be permitted to have an influence on you. You mark them in blue in your list. Do you like the idea?"

They loved it, but pointed out that they ended up with very few names in this first stage.

"Good, that's what it's all about," indicated Agustín, "you only fill your first circle with people who are worth having near."

SECOND CIRCLE OF ACTION

"In this circle you have to place all those people that you cannot distance yourself from and with whom you are obliged to coexist. They are people who you are tied to socially, like relatives, work mates or neighbours, amongst others. The effect of their behaviour on you has to be neutralized in your mind and in your feelings."

"But how?" asked Carmen.

"With mental discipline, repeating that you refuse to let them rob you of your taste for life and your happiness.

Your work with this circle has to lead you to effectiveness in your community labours. For example, if you don't really like your boss at work and you don't have the resources right now to change your job, first you neutralize his effect, or that of others who wear your energy, and second you learn to be effective in your job.

If you don't like your job, learn how to do it well. You turn it into a truthful lie and you carry it out in such a way that it looks as though you enjoyed it."

THIRD CIRCLE OF ACTION

"In the third circle you are going to place all those people who wear your energy, who are bad for you or who create an influence of mediocrity: those energetic vampires who systematically feed off your energy. The third circle of action is like a rubbish dump. Underline them in red in your list, and distance yourself from them without excuses."

"They are the majority of people in my list. Do I have to get rid of them?"

"Not exactly. First be sure about what you feel for each of these people and if it really does harm you to have their influence in your life, to confirm whether they belong to this group. If they do, get rid of them. If the opposite is true and if you love them, you don't have to stop loving them. On the contrary, you have to beautify and care for your relationship with each of them.

Eliminating the effects on us of the thoughts and opinions of others about our acts enables us to be the lords of our own destiny. It gives us wonderful freedom to choose what we want to think, feel and live.

For this strategy, the directive sentences that I have taught you are a guide for how to begin to learn to educate your thoughts and how to banish a thought that is no use and that corrodes and to replace it with another that is useful and strengthens.

But let's continue with the circles of action. There is a circle that I call 'Circle One and a Half', in which you place the people you love but who can be unbearable and conflictive, for example your partner. When your partner is wonderful, you enjoy him and you make him happy, and when he is unbearable you neutralize him and you are indifferent. At this point it is important that he doesn't see your indifference because he could take it as a form of passive aggression. He shouldn't find out what you are thinking under any circumstances.

If your partner criticizes you or tells you off for some stupid conflictive adolescent reason, you nod your head, as if you were saying he was right, you look at the floor and you say mentally 'nothing that my beloved partner says in this moment means anything to me...' or any other sentence that supports this idea, such as ' know my partner loves me', 'I refuse to believe that what he says is true', 'It's his belief, not mine, I refuse to take it on or believe it'.

This circle allows you to enjoy the people you love when the time is right and be indifferent when it is necessary."

Carmen couldn't totally accept this and she asked about the possibility of all the people she knew ending up in the second and third circles of action, and the first remaining empty.

"This situation," he explained with great patience, "teaches you how important it is to look after and cultivate the marvellous people that you have met in the world.

I'll make it clearer: of your list of 100 people, which of them would place you in their first circle?"

Carmen looked at the floor.

"I'll make it even worse. My apprentices should be in the first circle of Agustín - exquisite beings that one can have confidence in. What do you have, or do you think you have, for me to take you as an apprentice and put you in my first circle?

It is the teacher who chooses the pupil, for his energetic, psychic and spiritual capacity, but he has to be in this first circle of action. How will you get me to choose you? By becoming a first-rate woman."

FOURTH CIRCLE OF ACTION

"This is made up of people who aren't on your list of 100 people and is formed of all those people who you relate to occasionally and who you must treat with great decency and respect."

DIRECTIVE SENTENCES

Almost twenty years ago, when I was only fourteen years old, I worked with a book called "A Course of Miracles" by Helen Schucman and William Thetford. The experience inspired me to create the following system in which I borrow their marvellous method and add my own beliefs.

Following this process will enable you to rescue yourself. I have recreated from the original text the following sentences, which I call 'directive sentences' and which work miracles. They offer an indispensable support for the strategy of the Four Circles of Action, especially when dealing with energetic vampires.

Understand that I have tried to adapt my knowledge to Western understanding.

The objective is to restructure the states of alignment that we have been subjected to, to enjoy our right to be free and to choose what's best for us without stepping on the freedom of others. Respect for the liberty of others means leaving them in peace from our thoughts.

These 'directive sentences' constitute an option to re-educate your mind: you withdraw one mental programme and in its place you save a programme that constantly repeats shamanic principles.

I remind you that the human mind suffers the curse of forgetfulness: we very easily forget, only remembering that we once knew something. You have to repeat a concept over and over again until it is engraved in your consciousness.

We have to learn to transmute energy, to substitute worry for neutrality; fear for indifference; depression for marvel at our existence; loss of energy for vitality, and mental oppression with internal silence, always resorting to impeccability and the energy supplied by the Earth and the cosmos.

We have to build into our lives a cosmovision that takes us to controlled abandon and to incorporate the beauty of impeccability in all our acts.

METHOD

Each lesson should be carried out in phases of 5 to 30 minutes, between 3 and 5 times a day, for one or two days, or repeated in each period as many times as possible each day, trying to

155

understand and assimilate the concept, to situate it in the strategy of the four circles of action.

When you find a sentence that seems to resonate and proves useful, you should to repeat it to saturation point. When a sentence causes a feeling of rejection, it is a good idea to omit it and continue with the next.

It is very important that you don't believe anything, but at the same time reject nothing. Consider every sentence and try to find the reason why it vibrates in your consciousness in favour or against.

FIRST WEEK: UNCONCERN

Look for the flavour of every sentence. Revise it, repeat it slowly and try to understand it. Don't oblige yourself to understand: learn in a natural, relaxed way, breathe deeply and allow consciousness to enter you.

This process, carried out day after day, in numerical order, should take you to the point where self-reflection is completely stopped. What remains is exclusively your consciousness.

Consciousness isn't criticism. It is understanding and observing from an unconcerned, impartial analysis.

Write in the blank spaces the words or idea that you feel to be suitable to complete each sentence. They can be either objects situated around you or that come to mind in each moment.

1. ………………… (any object) means nothing to me.
2. ………………. (any object) is only an interpretation of my mind.………………… means nothing to me.
   By freeing myself of this interpretation I can re-establish my interpretation of the world as I like.
3. ………………… (any thought) means nothing to me.
   ………………… only exists in my mind. It is only an interpretation of my mind.
4. I transmute …………………(a feeling) into good luck.
   ………………. (a negative thought) means nothing to me. Out of me.
5. This feeling ………………. is energy that I learn to channel.
   I transmute this feeling ………………. into good luck.
   I transmute this feeling ………………. into consciousness.
   This feeling means nothing to me.
   6. If this object is an interpretation, what is real?
   I ask myself what this object is really like.
   I only see an interpretation of the past.

156

How many interpretations are there for any one object?

7. This thought .... (specify) isn't really as I see it. It is only an interpretation of my past.

I give things .... (specify) all the meaning they have for me. I have the freedom to choose.

SECOND WEEK: MY MYTH

Our way of perceiving reality hardens our vision of the world, limiting us to social egocentricity.

The shaman's apprentice little by little learns to choose the healthiest and most harmonious way of interpreting reality, discovering that variety exists at the time of choosing how we want to interpret the stimuli of the world.

Each shaman gives himself the task of converting his life into a myth, to reach beyond the aspirations offered by the social order, and to triumph.

8. I want to give new value to my interpretation of the world. I want to interpret the world according to my desires and the desires Spirit has for me. I want to interpret this life as if it was a marvellous place and I was a living myth. My myth is: ....

9. Emptiness is an energetic space in which I can place a new life. My option is to empty myself in order to fill myself again. My emptiness permits me to fill myself with what I want and to become my myth.

10. When I interpret what surrounds me I only see the past.

11. What I see is only the past, what the world wanted me to see. I now choose how I want to see the world. I want to see the world in this way ....
Above all, I want to see the world as it really is.

12. I don't see the world as it really is. I choose a suitable interpretation of the world for me. I really want to see the world in a different way. I want to perceive from the light side of reality, where I belong.

13. Harmony is the choice of my interpretation. My choice is to align myself with the harmonious side of reality.

14. Impeccability is the choice of my harmony. Impeccability is the energy I use to unite the world. Impeccability gives me the capacity to live the life I want to live.

157

THIRD WEEK: CHOICE

Impeccability and consciousness go hand in hand. Consciousness is neither stagnating in an egomaniacal vision, nor criticism of yourself or the world. Impeccability is the adequate use of energy, and consciousness is the correct interpretation of this energy.

Consciousness allows us to see how our internal machinery moves, what makes us routine and predictable, and it allows us to discover ways of stopping this machinery, whilst impeccability gives us enough energy to achieve it.

You can choose to perceive from the harmonious side of reality or to belong to the dark side of reality.

15. Harmony is my vision; impeccability is my gift.
16. Impeccability gives me the harmony I need to appreciate the world.
17. Impeccability is the energy I use to assemble the world.
18. This interpretation means nothing to me. This interpretation of the world .... is not my pact with Spirit. Do I really want to continue believing this?
19. Indifference banishes the interpretations that unbalance my world. Each day I find I am more and more indifferent to the interpretations arising from the dark side of reality; each day I am more and more indifferent to everything that distances me from harmony, balance and effectiveness.
20. This action has no importance but I act as though it did. This task .... has no value for me, but my impeccability leads me to do it so well and with such good results that it looks as though it were important to me.
21. Vision is my gift; impeccability is my right.

FOURTH WEEK: THE CONCEPT OF IMPECCABILITY

Let's try to understand the concept of impeccability a little better. Look for a synonym for 'impeccability' that you like and try to understand each sentence, but don't force yourself. Try to choose the sentence that best reaches you and wins the love of your consciousness.

· The suitable use of your energy
· No criticizing, neither internally nor externally
· Giving 100% in any act, and a little more
· Reaching the limit and going beyond to open your compartments and reserves of energy
· Acting in congruence with your pacts with God
· Giving the best of yourself, and a little bit more

158

- Finishing what you start, and doing it well and functionally
- Not permitting the predators of consciousness to devour you
- Not getting trapped in self-reflection, in "me, me, always me"
- Being discreet. Not telling the whole world who you are, what you do, how you feel, or how impeccable or good you are towards the world
- Your world and your impeccability are only for your eyes
- Impeccability is doing what you have to do in as little time as possible, with the best possible results and the least waste of energy
- The command of impeccability leads to a state of perfection with minimum effort

22. Impeccability is my gift. Cultivating impeccability is one of the most exquisite acts in this universe.
23. Impeccability is the adequate use of energy Does this situation .... give or take away energy from me? Do I really want to live this situation?
24. Impeccability is discretion, external silence. I don't tell everyone what I do, what I believe, who I am, what I feel, how Spirit manifests for me. It's only for my eyes and the eyes of God.
25. My impeccable acts are only for my eyes.
26. My impeccability is giving the best of myself, even though the situation means nothing. I am responsible for everything that I begin; therefore I am also responsible for finishing it well or for stopping doing it well.
27. I am indifferent to this problem, ... because my impeccability helps me to resolve it.
28. Indifference gives me sobriety, and impeccability offers me the precise way of facing an inconvenience. I am indifferent to this inconvenience ...., but although it doesn't matter to me, my impeccability demands that I give the best of myself in this situation.

FIFTH WEEK: TRANQUILLITY AND LIGHTNESS

Recognizing that a great part of the energy that we carry doesn't belong to us and that we are not obliged to take on the problems of others or global worries takes us to a point of reflection.

This point of reflection lightens our energy of the thoughts, energies and feelings that don't belong to us, enabling us in this way to redirect our life towards a life of plenitude.

29. There are no curses or blessings: life is a marvellous challenge.
30. Unconcern is a way of lightening the load of problems that don't belong to me. I don't worry about problems that don't belong to me: I don't think rubbish. I limit myself to taking on real situations that I can resolve.
31. There are no problems that belong to me. This problem .... is not mine, I don't have to carry it..., out of me. This problem means nothing to me; it has no power to unbalance my world.
32. I don't see problems in the world, only challenges to solve. This problem .... is not mine, my impeccability gives me another way to take it on, interpret it and resolve it in the best way possible.
33. I have no problems, only inconveniences that I am resolving. This problem does not suppose a waste of energy, it is a challenge to resolve, and impeccability gives me the vision of how my unconcern will give me the energy to resolve the inconvenience. It is easier and easier for me to resolve inconveniences.
34. Impeccability and unconcern give me energy to resolve my challenges.
35. Each challenge brings me a lesson and a gift. What can I learn from this event? I look for the best way to take advantage of a challenge.

SIXTH WEEK: POSITIVISM

The word has the power of infinite invocation; it is what sustains our vision of the world. We are what we think, and the world knows us according to what we say.

The apprentice learns to care for his words. Think about each sentence three times before you say it, don't say anything that you will later regret, and don't think or say rubbish.

36. Unconcern is easier and easier for me.
37. Every day I am lighter and lighter.
38. Every day I feel better and better.
39. Every day I am stronger. From this moment I am stronger and stronger.
40. Every day I have better control of my energy.
41. Every day it is easier for me to clean my links with Spirit.
42. Every day I have more personal power, more energy, and a

greater capacity for happiness.

SEVENTH WEEK: TRANSMUTATION

All energy can be transmuted and redirected.

Fear is only blocked energy, and this energy can be transmuted into good luck or any other positive situation.

Emotions are accompanied by thoughts, whilst feelings are associated with bodily manifestations. All physical feelings can be gently massaged with your hand while making a little invocation, towards the feeling that you want.

43. I have a lot of energy, but it is dispersed. From today I find it easier to redirect my energy.
44. My dispersed energy doesn't permit me to achieve my objectives. But every day it easier for me to achieve my objectives.
45. My dispersed energy clouds my thoughts. Every day it easier for me to achieve mental tranquillity.
46. My thoughts are confused because I don't know how to channel my energy. Impeccability opens the door to the adequate channelling of my energy.
47. My feelings of wear and tear disperse my energy. I liberate this feeling ………………. and I transform it into freedom.
48. My negative thoughts disperse my energy. I transmute these negative thoughts ………………. into good luck.
49. My blockages aren't bad. They are just obstructing my energy. I transmute this blockage ………………. into personal power. I convert this feeling in my body ………………. into good luck.

(Massaging the area where you experience the feeling)

EIGHTH WEEK: THE CONNECTION WITH
THE GREAT MOTHER CREATOR OF THE UNIVERSE

The connection with the Great Mother Creator of the Universe is the force that brings together consciousness and life; it is the power that governs our destiny.

That which you call God, I call the Great Mother Creator of the Universe. But the Great Mother Creator of the Universe is impersonal. She is neither good nor bad, she neither gives favours nor punishes anyone. The connection with the Great Mother Creator of the Universe only obeys personal power, and its corresponding mandates. All our work consists of cleaning our links to the connection with the Great Mother Creator of the Universe.

The connection to the Great Mother Creator of the Universe is called by means of the shine of the eyes, and mandates are

161

made through the energy of the womb, or the area two fingers width below the belly button.

50. Every day I find it easier to channel my energy.
51. The accumulation of free energy gives me personal power.
52. Personal power acts independently of reason.
53. Personal power acts according to my connection to the Great Mother Creator of the Universe. My discipline restores my personal power.
54. The connection to the Great Mother Creator of the Universe is the energy that harmonizes every personal universe.
55. My personal power takes me directly to the source, to the origin of harmony. I choose my interpretation of the world.
56. The connection to the Great Mother Creator of the Universe is the force with which I think. My essence is purity.

NINTH WEEK: FIRST REVISION

57. From lesson 1 to 7. This object .... means nothing to me. This object is only an interpretation of my mind. This thought means nothing to me. This feeling .... (negative) means nothing to me. It comes with me but it is not part of me, out of me... This feeling .... is energy that I learn to channel. I don't see this object .... as it really is... I only see an interpretation of the past. I give things .... all the meaning that they have for me.
58. Lesson 8 to 14. I don't understand the value of my interpretation. I see a world devoid of meaning. Emptiness is an energetic space in which I can place a new life. I only see the past. What I see is only the past; it is an interpretation that I have not chosen. I don't see the world as it really is. I choose an interpretation of the world that is suitable for me. Harmony is the choice of my interpretation. Impeccability is the choice of my harmony.
59. Lesson 15 to 21. Harmony is my vision. Impeccability is my gift. Impeccability gives me the harmony I need to appreciate the world. Impeccability is the energy I use to assemble the world. This interpretation means nothing to me. This interpretation of the world .... is not my pact with Spirit. Do I really want to continue believing this? Indifference banishes the interpretations that unbalance my world. This action has no importance but I act as though it did. Vision is my gift; impeccability is my right.
60. Lesson 22 to 28. Impeccability is my gift. Impeccability is the adequate use of energy. Impeccability is discretion, external silence. My impeccable acts are only for my eyes. My impec-

162

cability is giving the best of myself, even though the situation means nothing. I am indifferent to this problem, and I am practical when it is time to resolve it because my impeccability helps me to resolve it. Indifference gives me sobriety, and impeccability offers me the precise way of facing an inconvenience.

61. Lessons 29 to 35. There are no curses or blessings: life is a marvellous challenge. Unconcern is a way of lightening the load of problems that don't belong to me. I don't worry about problems that don't belong to me because I consider that to be thinking rubbish, I limit myself to taking on real situations that I can resolve. There are no problems that belong to me. I don't see problems in the world, only challenges to solve. I have no problems, only inconveniences that I am resolving. Impeccability and unconcern give me energy to resolve my challenges. Each challenge brings me a lesson and a gift. I look for the best way to take advantage of every challenge.

62. Lessons 36 to 42. Unconcern is easier and easier for me. Every day I am lighter and lighter. Every day I feel better and better. Every day I am stronger. Every day I have better control of my energy. Every day it is easier for me to clean my links with Spirit. Every day I have more personal power, more energy, and a greater capacity for happiness.

TENTH WEEK: SECOND REVISION

63. Lessons 43 to 49. I have a lot of energy, but it is dispersed. My dispersed energy doesn't permit me to achieve my objetives. My dispersed energy clouds my thoughts. My thoughts are confused because I don't know how to chanel my energy. Impeccability opens the door to adequate channelling of my energy. My feelings of waste disperse my energy. I convert this feeling into well-being and freedom. My negative thoughts disperse my energy. I transmute these negative thoughts into harmony. My blockages obstruct my energy. I transmute this blockage .... into personal power.

64. Lessons 50 to 56. Every day I find it easier to channel my energy. The accumulation of free energy gives me personal power. Personal power acts independently of reason. Personal power acts according to my connection to the Great Mother Creator of the Universe. My mental discipline restores my personal power. The connection to the Great Mother Creator of the Universe is the energy that harmonizes every personal universe. My personal power takes me directly to the source. I choose my interpretation of the world. The connection to the

163

Great Mother Creator of the Universe is the force with which I think. My essence is purity.

NEUTRALIZING

Little by little we begin to see the possibility of neutralizing the thoughts which overwhelm us or which waste our energy. On changing the quality of our thoughts, we change the quality of our life. This strengthens us as much in impeccability as in discipline.

Neutralizing the thoughts that waste our energy requires a true desire to overcome our habits and a battle to achieve emotional and mental well being.

This challenge has a cost, but it is payable and, if you don't begin today to pay the price of your happiness, the price of being able to choose the life you want to live and of your freedom, if you don't begin right in this moment, now that you have energy, strength and willpower, when will you do it?

65. There are thought that aren't mine: This thought. (specify) is not mine... I don't want it.
66. This thought belongs to .... (specify persona) and I respect it because it is his/hers, but I don't want it within my beliefs.
67. I don't want this thought about .... (specify) any more. I change it for a more harmonious thought.
68. This feeling .... is simply a loss of energy, it travels with me but it isn't part of me. I totally refuse to believe .... again. I am free of ....
69. The 'predators' are consciousnesses that feed off my energy; I can distinguish and neutralize them. I refuse to continue feeding them with my energy.

ELEVENTH WEEK: CONNECTION TO
THE GREAT MOTHER CREATOR OF THE UNIVERSE

The energy you are saving and your mental discipline take you to a state of amiable indifference, of gentle unconcern. They take you to a state of internal peace, where you discover that you are in control of your thoughts and feelings.

The people who know you won't understand this change and you will need to be very discreet in your use of these thoughts. The world has no reason to know what you are thinking, because it won't be able to understand it.

Here you begin to speak directly with the source, with your higher self, with the Great Mother, with Spirit, with the voice of seeing. You prepare your connection with the light side of reality in a methodical and harmonious way.

70. The connection with the Great Mother Creator of the Universe is the force that places things in the world for me to take.
71. The connection with the Great Mother Creator of the Universe permits me to take whatever I desire. My personal power allows me to recognize that I deserve it.
72. The connection with the Great Mother Creator of the Universe only obeys personal power.
73. My personal power is in harmony. My mind, my body and my feelings flow with my personal power. I only want what God wants, and God only wants what is best for me, which is what I want.
74. My connection with the Great Mother Creator of the Universe knows why I was born, what task I have to carry out on this plane.
75. My connection with the Great Mother Creator of the Universe permits me to harmonize my destiny with my experiences. It is living a life that is worth the trouble. My connection with the Great Mother Creator of the Universe is living the life that I have always wanted to live. It is living in harmony. My connection with the Great Mother Creator of the Universe is entering the sea of consciousness and paying the price of knowledge...
76. My connection with the Great Mother Creator of the Universe and myself are one.

TWELFTH WEEK: YOGUAL

The Yogual is the energetic body, the astral body, the soul, the dreaming body. When we sleep, our dreaming body leaves the physical body, without being conscious of its existence, just as from our physical plane we aren't conscious of our dreaming body.

Every night before getting into bed repeat mentally 'I am a dreamer, I am going to awake in a reality where....'

And on waking up, before getting out of bed, write about anything for five minutes.

77. My energy is divided in two, one part corresponds to my physical body and the other corresponds to my energetic body.
78. I find that I am divided into my physical body and yogual (dreaming body).
79. My physical body begins to remember my yogual and my

165

yogual ... begins to remember my physical body.

80. My accumulated consciousness allows my two bodies to recognize each other.

81. I am conscious that I am alive and that I am going to die. I am conscious that I have a physical body and a yogual. I am a dreamer.

82. Every day it is easier and easier to remember my dreams and the teachings that my yogual receives.

83. My apprenticeship grows in the consciousness of my yogual.

THIRTEENTH WEEK: CONSCIOUSNESS

Little by little we become conscious of the world and its manifestations, and we discover that the world is much more than we were told it was.

84. My consciousness opens to the unknown.

85. Consciousness is my gift.

86. Consciousness doesn't accept criticism, consciousness is understanding. I have the capacity to silence my mind and hear the voice of seeing.

87. Consciousness is not a rational process; it is absolute certainty experienced in my entire body.

88. Consciousness arrives to the seer. My nature is to see the essence of everything. The seer knows without knowing how he knows.

89. I accept no pacts other than my pacts with God, with Spirit or with the Infinite.

90. In everything I see, I see a past and an interpretation that I have not chosen. I neither recognize nor accept interpretations that I have not decided.

FOURTEENTH WEEK: SHAMANIC OBSERVATION

We begin to accumulate an inherent capacity to understand the world from the point of neutrality, which takes us to playing at being beyond good and bad. Therefore the world is not bad, but it is dangerous and people are not good, they are magical. Observation allows us to distance ourselves from the prejudices of justification and takes us to a point of joy and internal peace.

91. My capacity enables me to observe things without criticizing.

92. My personal power can make the world move in my favour.

93. My shamanic observation enables me to save energy and to know how to channel it.

94. There is no way that I will go back to criticizing myself. I can

166

only observe impartially the improvements that I have to make in my world. I only have nice, disciplined words for my apprenticeship and myself.

95. I want to, I can, I deserve to.
96. Shamanic observation takes me to contemplation, which permits me to live each moment in the present.
97. I am a shamanic observer.
98. I am a dreamer.
99. I am a seer and a shaman.

EPILOGUE

The shaman looked at the world from a cliff. The morning mist penetrated to his bones.

"I'm not as young as I was," he thought.

He looked at the book he held in his hands. He didn't know whether to publish it. He didn't know whether to burn it. He didn't know whether to throw it into he stream that was at the foot of the ravine that was below him.

He thought that his task was concluded with his first book, and he didn't know what to do with the second, the one that he had written for himself. He thought it would be a good idea if his apprentices had access to reading it in their dreams; that they should learn to steal his secrets, like first-rate shamans.

He decided to burn his second book. The idea relaxed him. He was sure that some of his apprentices would be able to rescue it in dreams. Slowly and ceremoniously he started a small fire.

He abandoned himself to the gentle pleasure of alleviating the coldness in his body with the fire. He placed the draft of the book on it. The flames, still small, seemed in no hurry to burn the document. His soul rested.

Lola approached slowly. She had come from the Casita, looking for Agustín. She brought with her a recently published volume of what was the shaman's first book. In silence she sat down next to him.

"Here it is, finally," Lola said to him. "Is that your new book?" she asked, looking at the document that seemed to fight to avoid being consumed by the flames.

"Yes," answered Agustín, "All my being knows that today I will burn my book. They are my memories of José."

Lola, very slowly, got up, put her hands in the fire and removed the document that the flames were beginning to catch, and placed the one she had brought with her in its place.

"So be it," she said with resolution.

"You are only a dream," said Agustín smiling. He knew in that moment that Spirit was manifesting. And he also knew his immediate destiny⋯ But he wasn't going to reveal it right now to her, even thought they were totally in the ether.

He smiled in the knowledge that Spirit had rescued his memories of José through Lola. José's soul had manifested as his memories were recovered from the fire. Agustín knew that the book wasn't entirely his.

"Spirit loves you very much," assured Lola as she put out the fire on the edges of the volume she had just rescued from the fire.

"And you too," Agustín looked at her with deep love and respect, while the first book was consumed by the fire. He truly considered himself a happy man.

Can Armenteras, September, 2001.

APPENDIX 1
OLLIN YOLIZTLI AND SCHOOL OF LIFE

10% of the profits from the sale of this book go to the Foundations Ollin Yolitzli and School of Life.

OLLIN YOLIZTLI (MOVEMENT AND LIFE)

Founded by Efren Delagdo Orea (Agustín), in support for humanity and our beautiful world, the Foundation Ollin Yoliztli (a registered charity based in Spain) works to combine the best the western world has to offer with the best of the spiritual world.

"Our love for Spirit and humanity, our desire to learn and search, our efforts towards building a bridge between consciousness and knowledge, between happiness and perception, our efforts to improve ourselves, all lead us to growth and to help others to grow.

We are not here in this beautiful life only to receive; we also need to give to those who - like us - are hungry for knowledge.

As a Foundation, our efforts are channelled into finding new and better ways of serving humankind. In order to grow ourselves, and to help you grow, we need your support."

Agustín

To find out more about Ollin Yoliztli, and the activities offered, please visit the website www.ollinyoliztli.org.

SCHOOL OF LIFE

School of Life (SoL) is an international charity registered in Spain, working in the fields of environment, health, the arts, faith, economics and conflict resolution to inspire people to actively participate in the movement towards the creation of a positive future for the planet and ourselves.

SoL focuses on providing the education people need to make informed choices, building a network of different organisations and individuals finding positive and innovative ways of working towards the common goal of a sustainable future.

The main educational focus is the creation of an innovative one-year full-time training programme which will train a new kind of professional - the Sustainability Designer, capable of measuring the impact of human activity on all areas of human culture and promoting sustainable values such as awareness, responsibility, creativity, integrity, etc.

For more information about the project, and courses and activities on offer, please visit the web page at www.school-of-life.net, or write to us on mail@school-of-life.net.

SoL's initiative, School of Life Press, furthers the work towards a sustainable future for all by promoting individual work for transformation and growth on every level. The annual list is selected from the understanding that each individual can release personal issues and find balance within themselves, and in this way we can collectively influence the movement of energy on the planet. School of Life Press will focus initially on books in the area of personal and spiritual growth, and starts their list with the publishing of The Key to the Universe - a Toolkit from the School of Life (ISBN 84-607-9107-6, priced £16.99.) and The Shaman's Garden: Memories Stolen from the Dead Stars - A Branch of Toltec Shamanism (ISBN 84-609-1035-0, priced £9.99).

APPENDIX 2
WORKSHOPS, COURSES AND RETREATS

WORKSHOPS

Agustín offers a programme of weekend workshops in many different locations in Europe. Some of the workshops are offered in Spanish, while others are translated into English and/or German. To find out more about his current schedule, visit the web page www.familiazul.com, or send a mail to shamanism@school-of-life.net.

Among the weekend Workshops on offer are:
Introduction to Shamanism - The Dance with Death
Falling in Love with Life - The Album of Sublime Moments
Healing - The Fire Snake
The Art of Stalking
The Art of Dreaming
The Warrior's Promise

INTENSIVE COURSES

At Christmas, Easter and in July and August, Agustín offers intensive courses in La Casita, his house in Northern Spain. These courses are translated into German and/or English. To find out about the current programme, visit the web page www.familiazul.com, or send a mail to shamanism@school-of-life.net.

"In our lineage, perhaps the true doorway to the path of knowledge is offered in the work we do in La Casita de Armenteras. These intensive courses offer the flavour of plenitude, beauty and energy. A unique state of consciousness is created through joy and the resurgence of the soul, body and mind.

Each intensive course covers a specific theme and the exact dynamics, exercises and rituals vary according to the energy of the people who participate.

What happens in these intensive courses is difficult to explain with words: it is a pure experience.

> The Blue Path
> is the Path of Knowledge.
> It is a path of love,
> Of the search for consciousness.
> We hunt joy and triumph,
> And we serve Spirit and Humanity.
> We meet in the ceremony
> Of joy and plenitude.
> Here in Armenteras
> Life is intensity,
> Beauty and friendship."
>
> *Agustín*

RETREATS AND 'SHAMANASTERY'

At Christmas, Easter and in the summer months, La Casita, Agustín's house in Northern Spain, is open to people who want to spend some time experiencing the innovative concept of the 'shamanastery'. This concept of 'active rest' in a beautiful rural environment involves paying a small amount for your food and accommodation, working in service to the house in the mornings, with talks, walks, drumming, fires, energy work etc, in the early mornings, afternoons and evenings. To find out more visit www.armenteras.com or send a mail to shamanism@school-of-life.net.

> "Love is the glue
> With which we unite Healing.
> Joy
> Drums
> The fire in the tipi
> The walks in the woods
> Friendship.
> Life nurtures
> Consciousness unites
> This and more is the Shamanastery
> In Armenteras."
>
> *Agustín*

ABOUT THE AUTHOR

Itzcoatl Papalotzin is writer, poet, painter, musician, dancer, businessman, speaker and Man of Knowledge. He has trained in Social Anthropology and Neuro-Linguistic Programming. He has worked with many American shamans, among them Huichol, Mayan, Lakota, Apache and indigenous peoples of the Amazon, as well as with Maoris of New Zealand and Tibetan monks from the Shartse Monastery in India.

He is the founder of Ollin Yoliztli (Life and Movement), a foundation that seeks to create a space where the best of the Western world can be combined with the best of spiritual philosophy. His life has been about finding balance between his mysticism and the beliefs of the western world, achieving plenitude and inner peace, relating in harmony and love with each of the people who share his social environment. He began giving courses when he was 22 years old, and has been teaching his particular way of understanding reality ever since, in Mexico, the USA, New Zealand, South America, and more recently in several countries in Europe, among them Spain, Austria, Switzerland, Germany and Italy.

Born in Mexico, he prefers to think of himself as an inhabitant of the third planet of our solar system. He has had many names: Edgar, Agustín, Bear Foot, Efren, but his name within the Nahuatl tradition of Mexico is Ce Acatl Topinzin Itzcoatl Papalotzin, the name José gave him the day he told him that Spirit had signalled him as an apprentice. The name means Two Canes, Pebble, Obsidian Snake, Lord Butterfly; but he prefers to call himself Obsidian Butterfly Snake.

Agustín, as he is known in Europe, considers himself to be a servant of Spirit: he lives by Spirit, for Spirit, in Spirit, and he has taken care to have the most upright life possible, always offering an example, both in acts and words. Itzcoatl Papalotzin offers you a path that enables you to walk through your life in a state of happiness and inner struggle, a way of achieving the correct way to live, where magic combines with well-being.

ABOUT THE TRANSLATOR

Joanna Crowson was born in Yorkshire. She spent much of her childhood in Canada before returning to the UK in her teens. She is a graduate in English Literature and History of Art, from the University of Kent at Canterbury. She has had many jobs in the UK, from teaching home maintenance to women, to running a wholefood shop, to standing for the Green Party in local elections. 14 years ago, in a spirit of adventure, she left Britain with her partner and their 2 children aged 1 and 5 in an ancient land rover called Lilly. They bought land on the Costa de la Luz, founded a cooperative language school and self-built Casa Gaia, their ecological home. Her varied life experiences have led to her involvement with School of Life where she is Director and Member of the Board. She lives in Cádiz with her family, which now includes various dogs, cats, chickens and voluntary workers. She is a writer, co-author with Silja Winther of The Key to the Universe: A Toolkit from the School of Life, a translator, and teacher within the Blue Lineage of Toltec shamanism, offering joy as a path of knowledge and wisdom.

OTHER BOOKS PUBLISHED BY SCHOOL OF LIFE PRESS

The Key to the Universe
A Toolkit from the School of Life
Joanna Crowson
Silja Winther
Paintings by Katrina Vrebalovich

The Key to the Universe is presented in a beautiful box containing:
paperback book, 153 pages
53 full colour cards

ISBN 84-607-9107-6
£16.99

The book presents a new energetic system for understanding human growth and spiritual development: Star of 13. Together, the book and cards offer a toolkit that helps you connect to the Primal Energies and begin working on them in your everyday life. Through conscious integration of these Energies you can work on problem areas of your life and relationships, save energy wasted in meaningless repetitions, and channel it into achieving your objectives. There are many paths you can explore that can lead you to growth: here is one that enables you to take practical steps to improve your daily life, the life of those around you and the future of the planet.

"...The Key to the Universe is a contemporary women's expression of ancient esoteric principles, retold artistically through oracle cards and a luminous text that informs and guides the seeker with ideas and suggestions that make sense. A work of love."
Vicki Noble, author of Motherpeace Tarot and Shakti Woman

For more information about the book and the energetic system Star of 13 - The Primal Energies, visit the website *www.thekeytotheuniverse.com*. You will find information about the system, sample artwork, extracts from the book and an on-line oracle.